D0160746

Mary Virginia Robinson
– November 1989.

Wildflowers Across America

Lady Bird Johnson
and Carlton B. Lees

Photographs Selected by Les Line

National Wildflower Research Center
Abbeville Press · Publishers · New York

Editor Walton Rawls
Designer James Wageman
Production Supervisor Hope Koturo

Library of Congress Cataloging in Publication Data
Johnson, Lady Bird, 1912–
Wildflowers across America / by Lady Bird Johnson and Carlton Lees; photographs selected by Les Line.
p. cm.
Bibliography: p.
Includes index.
ISBN 0-89659-770-9. ISBN 0-89659-866-7 (collector's ed.)
1. Wild flowers—United States. 2. Wild flowers—United States—Pictorial works. 3. Botany—United States—History. 4. Plant collectors—United States. 5. Plant conservation—United States. 6. Urban beautification—United States. 7. Roadside improvement—United States. I. Lees, Carlton B. II. Title.
QK115.J63 1988 *88-1275*
582.13'0973—dc19 *CIP*

Inquiries should be addressed to Abbeville Press, Inc., 488 Madison Avenue, New York 10022. Printed and bound in Japan. First edition, fourth printing.

I

Mexican poppy *(Eschscholtzia mexicana),* New Mexico. ROBERT P. CARR

2/3

Pink monkeyflowers, lupine, asters, and Queen Anne's lace *(Mimulus lewisii, Lupinus perennis, Aster laevis, Daucus carota),* Washington. PAT O'HARA

4/5

Mountain rosebay *(Rhododendron catawbiense),* North Carolina. DAVID MUENCH

Contents

Foreword

The Constitution of the United States does not mention the First Lady. She is elected by one man only. The statute books assign her no duties; and yet, when she gets the job, a podium is there if she cares to use it. I did. The public nature of the White House allowed me to focus attention on the environment, especially on plantings for roadsides and parks. But my story begins long before that—with a love of the land that started in my childhood.

Almost every person, from childhood on, has been touched by the untamed beauty of wildflowers: buttercup gold under a childish chin, the single drop of exquisite sweetness in the blossom of wild honeysuckle, the love-me, love-me-not philosophy of daisy petals.

*I grew up in the country—rather alone—and one of my favorite pastimes was to walk in the woods, exploring, particularly in the springtime, searching for the first wild violets and starry white blossoms of dogwood, feeling the crush of pine needles underfoot, the wind whispering overhead. In summer, barefoot with sand between my toes, I hunted for the Cherokee rose and the black-eyed Susans that grew along the fence rows. Still vivid in my thoughts is Caddo Lake, with Spanish moss draped from age-old cypresses, dark, enchanting lagoons, where occasionally you would see an alligator slithering down a muddy bank. In Alabama where I spent my vacations with Aunt Effie and my cousins, I remember the wild mountain laurel (*Kalmia latifolia*) that grew in the pinewoods, its clusters of pale pink flowerets freckled with tiny brown spots.*

Wrinkled rose
(Rosa rugosa),
Maine.
LES LINE

Flowering dogwood
(Cornus florida),
North Carolina.
PAT O'HARA

In 1930, I went to Austin to attend the University of Texas. West and south of Austin, after you cross the Balcones escarpment, the countryside is a land of chalky hills, clear streams, and crooked live oak trees. In the early spring, all the roadsides and pastures and the virgin fields of this Texas Hill Country were covered with bluebonnets. As the season deepened into summer, a Persian carpet of Indian-blanket and paintbrush and coreopsis replaced the bluebonnets, while purple thistles and sunflowers began to appear. Even the campus of the university, especially the long hill down from the old main building, was strewn with wildflowers.

Back in those days, I delighted in going on picnics and explorations in the spring. There were plenty of like-minded friends, mostly girls (and boys who went because we did). We would search and find, and walk and take pictures, and have picnics. It was a lovely time! I have some pictures of those days—old and faded now—with me lying in a field of bluebonnets. Oddly enough, I came across such a picture of my granddaughter Rebekah made about forty-five years later in a similar field of bluebonnets!

Since then, my life has taken me to many areas of the United States. I think of walking down a quiet lane in Martha's Vineyard, bordered by tangles of pink wild roses, with a cloud of daisylike white blossoms frosting the meadows, or of strolling a forest path beside a crystal stream in the Callaway Gardens of Georgia and being stopped still by a heady blaze of wild orange-red azaleas against the forest's emerald green. In New Mexico in September, I saw golden aspen climbing the hillsides and wild purple asters dotting the roadsides. I have always been a natural tourist; Lyndon used to say I kept "one foot in the middle of the big road." Wherever I go in America, I like it when the land speaks its own language in its own regional accent.

In 1964, when Lyndon ran for the presidency, we traveled the campaign trail together to every corner of the country. Demanding, exhausting best describe those "twenty-eight-hour days"—but that dimension was far exceeded by the exhilaration of seeing more of this great land.

During that campaign, we both were thinking very deeply in our hearts about the things we could do to fulfill our aspirations for the nation. For me, those aspirations were shaped by my longtime love of nature, reinforced by seeing the vastness of this land—its beauty and its blight. Our eyes frequently met the majesty of America's splendor, but, sadly, all too often the evidence of neglect and abuse.

Black-eyed Susan *(Rudbeckia hirta)*, Connecticut. LES LINE

Mountain laurel *(Kalmia latifolia)*, Connecticut. LES LINE

Yellow flax (*Linum rigidum*), paintbrush (*Castilleja* sp.), and Texas bluebonnets (*Lupinus texensis*), Texas. JOHN SHAW

Although education, civil rights, and health were high on Lyndon's agenda for his administration, the environment also claimed his efforts from the earliest days of his presidency. In an address soon after his election, he said:

> *We have always prided ourselves on being not only America the strong and America the free, but America the beautiful. Today that beauty is in danger. The water we drink, the food we eat, the very air we breathe are threatened with pollution. Our parks are overcrowded and our seashores overburdened. Green fields and dense forests are disappearing. A few years ago we were concerned about the Ugly American. Today, we must act to prevent an Ugly America. For once the battle is lost, once our natural splendor is destroyed, it can never be recaptured. And once man can no longer walk with beauty or wonder at nature, his spirit will wither, and his sustenance be wasted.*

In years past, I had not given any conscious thought to taking a hand in preserving our natural heritage or to heightening its beauty—except in our family surroundings. Gardening in my own backyard in Washington had brought me much pleasure. I remember planting a weeping cherry, a pink dogwood, and a crab apple to make a quadrangle with the old apple tree already growing there. Laughingly I told my husband that my epitaph would be "She planted three trees!"

When I found myself in the White House, it was natural—and inevitable—for me to turn to the movement we called beautification (we never could think of a better word!). Because my heart had for so long been in the environment, I began to think that in the White House I might now have the means to repay something of the debt I owed nature for the enrichment provided from my childhood onward. And since hometown for the next few years was still to be Washington, D. C., where better to start than in "the nation's front yard"?

In February of 1965, Secretary of the Interior Stewart Udall and I gathered up a group of philanthropists, designers, publishers, officials, and civic leaders of many talents and persuasions to form the Committee for a More Beautiful Capital. Among the original members were officeholders whose jobs concerned the city of Washington, such as Mrs. James Rowe of the National Capital Planning Commission, Walter Washington of the National Capital Housing Authority (later mayor of the District of

Flame azalea *(Rhododendron calendulaceum)*, North Carolina. PAT O'HARA

Columbia), and Nathaniel Owings, chairman of the President's Commission on Pennsylvania Avenue; and personal friends, such as Mrs. Albert Lasker, a philanthropist from New York. We were joined by a team of observers, including Laurance Rockefeller, whose intelligence and financial resources were devoted to beautification and conservation.

A companion philanthropic organization, called the Society for a More Beautiful National Capital, Inc., was also established, to serve as a clearinghouse for private donations—gifts to revitalize parks, equip playgrounds, construct fountains, support youth employment, and stimulate significant public and business investments. Gifts ranged from $2 sent by a soldier in Vietnam, to $14 from a visiting group of high school students, to $388,000 from the Vincent Astor Foundation to construct a community plaza.

The committee began by adopting hundreds of the small traffic triangles and circles (L'Enfant's wonderful legacy to the city), and guided by the philosophy of Mary Lasker, one of our most effective champions, we planted "masses of flowers where the masses pass." We encouraged businesses to landscape; organized clean-up, fix-up projects in neighborhoods; and sought to improve school yards and playgrounds. Bus tours throughout the city gave us a close-up look at what needed to be done. To this day, I never board a bus without thinking of our committee!

Widespread community participation was deemed essential for any lasting success. To attract that participation, we sponsored annual awards in three categories: public spaces, commercial properties, and neighborhoods. The honorees, including hundreds of children, were invited to the White House to receive these awards.

We tried to convey the importance of each individual's role in reducing litter, planting trees and flowers, and caring for his surroundings. This was something the ordinary citizen could do to change the looks of the world around him.

Beautification and revitalization can unite a city. And their by-products are many: economic growth, old-fashioned neighborliness, and a lift of spirit and heart that comes with new pride in yourself and what you have done with your surroundings.

On one of our beautification field trips, I remember coming upon a ravine in a Washington suburb. It was filled with rotting tires, junked refrigerators, discarded chunks of cement—all the debris of a careless civilization. In a year's time that scene changed. Citizen action raised the money to haul away forty truckloads of junk, to landscape, and to plant. That gully was transformed into an outdoor living room where old people sit under shade trees and children enjoy the sturdy playground equipment.

Some members of our committee helped organize thirty-seven blocks in a low-income neighborhood. They persuaded merchants to contribute $3,400 worth of paint, brushes, rakes, shovels, and brooms to the cause. One summer week a thousand boys and girls and two hundred adults were enlisted to clean out the trash. Sixty-five truckloads were hauled away!

Some of our efforts were concentrated on relieving the institutional look of the public schools, most of which did not have a bush or sprig of grass to soften the masonry. I remember visiting one particular school at the start of the program and counting twenty-six broken windows. In 1965, broken school windows cost the District budget over $118,000. In New York City, the cost was then about $1 million per year. We enlisted the help of nurseries. We asked local foundations and generous donors to help, and science teachers and art teachers brought the children into the effort. A new pride reduced vandalism. Each deed opened the eyes of the community to fresh needs and fresh opportunities for improving the physical environment of the city. We wanted Washington to be a model for cities throughout the land.

That capable committee helped write a marvelous chapter in Washington's life simply by improving on what was already there. Among the committee's accomplishments were the landscaping of hundreds of park sites and schools and playgrounds; the planting of nearly two million bulbs, 83,000 spring-flowering plants, 50,000 shrubs, 25,000 trees, and 137,000 annuals; the landscaping of several major thoroughfares and freeways into the city; and innumerable clean-up, fix-up, plant-up campaigns in depressed parts of the District.

To the public eye, what endures most from these years is drifts of yellow daffodils along the Potomac and in Rock Creek Park, and brilliant seasonal changes of color in the many triangles and squares.

Though the word beautification *makes the concept sound merely cosmetic, it involves much more: clean water, clean air, clean roadsides, safe waste-disposal, and preservation of valued old landmarks as well as great parks and wilderness areas. To me, in sum, beautification means our total concern for the physical and human quality we pass on to our children and the future.*

Indian blanket *(Gaillardia pulchella)* and coreopsis *(Coreopsis tinctoria)*, Texas.
JIM BONES

I remember so well one afternoon meeting with Walter Reuther of the AFL-CIO to enlist his support for legislation on parks and green spaces. He told me about the mental and emotional toll that assembly-line work brings upon the factory worker. "Most blue-collar workers don't have the money to fly off to the scenic places of the world," he said. "We need to bring the beautiful places close to home."

It is helpful, of course, for a First Lady with a cause to have a husband who believes in it, too. With encouragement and guidance, Lyndon was with me every inch of the way. An awareness began to blossom of the threats to our whole environment. Early legislation on water and air pollution, on clean rivers, on highway beautification, and on the preservation of wilderness areas is a proud part of those years.

This was a heady time for me, a cram course in park and land use, in city planning, and in the natural beauty of this diverse country. And while those days are long past, it is a cause I can never put down. I am living on a smaller stage now. My support as a citizen is all I can give to whatever efforts are made for the cause of natural beauty. It makes my heart sing to have a hand in helping the spot in the world where I happen to live to rise to its potential.

Flowering dogwood *(Cornus florida)*, New York.
LES LINE

When we came home to Texas from Washington in 1969, I felt that recognition was long overdue for the work of the Texas Highway Department. Beautification and preservation were long a part of the Texas highway tradition. I had observed this, was grateful for it, and had enjoyed it for many years.

The Texas beautification program actually began in 1929, when Judge W.R. Ely, a member of the Highway Commission, called for landscaped roadsides, with construction planned to retain natural beauty. Engineers were urged to preserve all the trees and plants they could when laying out the highways. The department persuaded neighboring ranchers or farmers to give an extra acre to establish turnouts for delightful little roadside parks. There was a respect for beauty, an encouragement of it.

I thought I ought to meet some of the men who actually do the job along our highways, to thank them for preserving one of wildflowers' last citadels. I have learned well that when springtime brings forth wildflowers along the roadsides, it is because a maintenance foreman had the foresight to hold off mowing until after the plants had gone to seed the year before, and then to have spread the hay-mulch of seeds on bare spots where there were no flowers.

To recognize the importance of the Texas foremen and their crews, I host a barbecue each fall at the LBJ State Park across from the ranch and give several modest awards to salute the most outstanding achievements. The top brass of the Texas Highway Department are, of course, invited. We have country music, an amusing skit, friends interested in the environment, and all the members of the press we can garner in order to spread the word and encourage the public to applaud the winners, too. Our judges are outstanding landscape professionals and civic leaders. They review scrapbooks of entries from each of the twenty-five highway districts in Texas, and the pictures show how each foreman has added beauty and welcome to his section of the highway.

Another project also has its roots in the environmental "vineyard." In my other favorite capital city, Austin, I have been involved in a project to enhance the river-front. It began in 1970, with the mayor and a committee of citizens. Along several miles of Town Lake, the river-front where the city owns the land, we have built hike and bike trails landscaped with mostly hardy native trees and plants, so there is a succession of color throughout the seasons—redbud, pear, and peach trees in early spring, a profusion of wildflowers in April and May (given enough rain), crepe-myrtles during long, hot summers, the deep red of Spanish oak and the copper of cypress for fall.

Any sunny day you can see that riverside in joyous use! Canoes dot the river, kites fly overhead; there are bicyclists, joggers, fishermen, young and old, and families picnicking in the shade of the trees lining the river.

It has become a project that belongs to the whole community. Pride in it has led to gifts from individuals in memory of loved ones or to mark a special milestone, and to gifts from banks and businesses that think it makes good corporate sense to enrich their city. The river-front is one of the "trademarks" of Austin; when the city is on television, you are shown scenes of the capitol building, the University of Texas Tower, and a portion of Town Lake.

As I worked on these projects, the idea of a research center for native American plants went tantalizingly around in my mind. I talked with experts about what could and what should be done. And finally I decided that, in this happy hour of my life, this would be the project I would give my time and energies to.

We have impressive and valid reasons for using our native plants—reasons of the soul and of the pocketbook. Why, then, aren't we putting this resource to more

(Top) Lady Bird Johnson and former President Lyndon B. Johnson with award winners at the 1970 Texas Highway Beautification Awards ceremony at the LBJ Ranch. FRANK WOLFE (Bottom) Mrs. Johnson addressing the Texas Highway Beautification Awards guests on October 2, 1970. FRANK WOLFE

(Top) Lady Bird Johnson speaking to the crowds attending the Town Lake Dedication Ceremony in Austin, Texas, on December 10, 1971. FRANK WOLFE (Bottom) The Jamie Odum Pavilion at Lou Neff Point, in Phase III of the Town Lake Development in Austin. PAUL CHEVALIER

widespread use? The barrier is insufficient knowledge! We simply do not possess enough reliable information about germination requirements and growth patterns to ensure consistent and predictable results. The growing of wildflowers is certainly not an exact science, as anyone who has tried will tell you. I have planted bluebonnet seeds and gotten some fine bluebonnets—and also a large abundance of invading grasses. Nor do we know how best to blend a succession of wildflowers into landscape management plans for all seasons. Seeds are another difficulty. They are expensive. If the demand increases, certainly less costly ways of harvesting will be developed, and the price will go down.

So, on my seventieth birthday, in 1982, I "threw my hat over the windmill" and celebrated by giving sixty acres of land on the Colorado River just outside Austin and enough seed money to found the National Wildflower Research Center. We will save most of that story for later, but in brief: The Center is an officially chartered, nonprofit corporation with a vigorous, enthusiastic board of trustees from all over the country, aided by a band of dedicated volunteers. My cochairman is the actress and wildflower lover Helen Hayes, who lives in New York. Carlton Lees was one of my earliest partners. Dr. David Northington is our director and one of the nation's top experts on the nomenclature and ecology of wildflowers and other native plants. Nash Castro, executive director of the Palisades Interstate Park Commission, New York and New Jersey, is our founding president.

The Center's goals are national and ambitious: to learn as much as we can about wildflower propagation and growth and to be a clearinghouse to spread that knowledge to developers, park managers, and private citizens everywhere.

This is a pioneering effort, and sometimes I feel overwhelmed with a sense of so much to do and so little time, because of all we need to discover. Yet I can hardly wait for spring each year! Already we are on the road to unlocking some of the secrets of wildflowers and to assuring their bounty in our landscapes for generations to come.

Do I want to "tame" wildflowers? I would be annoyed and immediately launch into a denial if anybody asked me that. I hope *that is not what I want. But I yearn to* learn *about them and to get more reliable, consistent, predictable results when planting them.*

Working together—sharing our experiences—we shall succeed.

From the American Scene: Natives and Immigrants

Wildflower Adventures

A Pink Hill of Evening Primrose

Pink evening primrose *(Oenothera speciosa),* Texas. LARRY WEST

Pink evening primrose, Texas. DAVID MUENCH

The spring of 1984 was not a good season for wildflowers in the Hill Country of central Texas. Our average rainfall of 28 to 30 inches per year is all too apt to turn into 18 inches one year—meager, paltry—or a glorious 45 inches the next year. This had been a dry year. Even so, I went out in the car with a friend one morning in early April, taking my sun-hat, the camera, and some old beat-up flat shoes, just to see what we could see. It was impossible to set out under a clear, blue sky with fleecy white clouds and not have a certain feeling of buoyancy, elation! What would the day hold? So we drove along, and the landscape unfolded in front of us—farmland, rolling hills, meadows, plains. I often think the roadside is the last refuge of wildflowers, because "the plow and the cow" don't get to them along the right-of-way.

But in this dry year, there were very few flowers to be seen. Mile after mile and half-hour after half-hour passed, and I was beginning to feel a little daunted. Suddenly, off to the left I saw a rising hill of pink—an unbelievably beautiful carpet of exquisite pink, a sort of Marie Laurencin shade. I said to the driver (so quickly that I must have alarmed him), "Stop!" He came to a halt, and I saw a lane, a little dirt *road, ascending toward the top of a hill where a house was under construction. We turned up this road, and on our left everything was a sheer glorious pink; on the right a barbed-wire fence guarded a rough, brown field. Apparently no shredder had been through the previous fall after the vegetation turned brown, so what you saw mostly was a scruffy bunch of dried, brown thatch with some green pushing through and only a few of the pink flowers that grew so profusely on the left. It was evening primrose (*Oenothera speciosa*)—to me one of the most exquisite and feminine of all wild-flowers!*

Across the fence, in the middle of the brown field, I saw a huge behemoth, a Goliath of a tractor, coming at us down the hill like an engine of war. I jumped out of the car, marched up to the fence—quite without the slightest right to do so—and began to call "Stop!" to the young man who was driving the tractor. Then I began to wave my hat to attract his attention, because with that much noise he couldn't pay me any mind. Moreover, I was an intruder on his own land. He ground to a halt right close to me and said, "Yes, ma'am?" That was a good sign. "Ma'am" always puts an elderly Southern lady more at her ease. He was clear-faced, big, strong, a nice-looking young man. I asked "Son, does this land belong to you?" And he said, "No, ma'am, to my father." I introduced myself and told him why I was interested and asked, did he suppose his father might possibly just rent me the hill—at least until these flowers went to seed so we could try harvesting them. He looked at me with the funniest look. I think he thought I was just some kind of daffy city person who didn't know what she was talking about.

He was quite right! I didn't know anybody who had ever harvested the seeds of Oenothera speciosa. *How would you get the seeds out, and how would you go about planting them? But I yearned to take the chance. He said, "My father lives in San Marcos. Do you want me to write his phone number down?" I sure did, and then asked, "Do you mind if we just walk up and down your lane and through the flowers, if we're careful?" He answered, "No, go right on, help yourselves." We brought along the camera and we took pictures of ourselves standing up and sitting down. There was an especially thick and lovely clump of flowers with a little half-bare space in between where I sat down hoping there were no sticker burrs—as there often were in those fields. There were also a few little white daisylike flowers and more than a few yellow ones. We just took our fill of pictures and finally got up and bid the young man good-bye.*

Pink evening primrose *(Oenothera speciosa)*, paintbrush *(Castilleja* sp.*)*, and Texas bluebonnets *(Lupinus texensis)*, Texas.
DAVID MUENCH

Little else did that day yield. There was not the spring glory that we wanted. But we saw that this flower, this evening primrose, could survive (could even flourish and be magnificent!) with a very few inches of rain. Now, was this a one-time thing? Do oenothera like dry springtimes? Why should there be so many on that hill and not massed anywhere else around? All of this intrigued me. And if we came back year after year, would that pink glory always be there?

I would love to spend some of the remaining days the Lord gives me trying to solve such things, and I wanted to get those seeds out of those pods to put them someplace where the flowers could be viewed and admired by lots of people.

Well, I did get in touch with the father of the young man, and he said, "Just come get all you want." I said, "No, I really want to know what you are going to do with that land so I won't inconvenience you, because your son's plowing it right now. Will you let me rent it through April, May, June, and July? I feel sure I can harvest those seeds in June or July." (I was not feeling sure at all.) And he said, "I guess I could hold off on my winter oats. August is a pretty good time to plant them, turning up the soil in August and maybe planting the first of September if we get some rain" (the constant refrain of this land). I said, "All right," and pulled a figure out of my hat. "You've got twenty-six acres here. Would you lease it to me for two hundred fifty dollars?" He paused a moment. I believe he, too, must have thought I was daffy, and he didn't want to take advantage of somebody out of her wits. But I insisted, and he said yes, and then I made out a check.

I got in touch with the only person I knew who harvested seed (other than bluebonnet seed, for many people do that). No, he had never harvested any of this kind, but he said he sure would like to try. So, the result was that he harvested them, and he discovered that this plant grows from an underground rhizome and pops up six inches, a foot, or eighteen inches away from where it starts out. The propagation actually comes from seeds in tiny hard-as-leather pods. I have not satisfactorily been able to break open those pods and get out the seed except by hand, which is too labor-intensive and absolutely beyond sanity for a large planting—and we wanted a field of it! So, in a few months, we had the wildflower hay-mulch—vines, little stalks, stems, a few faded blossoms, seed pods, withered leaves—great big sacks full of it! The harvester brought the hay-mulch over, and scattered it where we hoped the flower would grow.

This little vignette has two postscripts. First, when we went to lunch—on the day I discovered the hill of flowers—at an ice cream and hamburger place nearby, I reached for my glasses and they were not there! Had I left them in the field of evening primrose when I sat down for pictures? It was maddening and frustrating, because I am helpless without glasses, but it was farther to retrace our steps than to continue to other destinations. The day beckoned and we drove on.

I was determined, however, to pass by the field again before the season waned, to see "my crop." A week or so later, we stopped the car at the spot I thought I remembered, and, rather tremulously, I walked again into the pink sea looking for a bare spot where I recalled sitting down for pictures. There, gloriously, my lost glasses lay, primly folded and unharmed! I picked them up and went off, remembering Browning's lines about Pippa: "The year's at the spring/And day's at the morn; . . . /The hill-side's dew-pearled; . . . /All's right with the world!"

And now the other postscript: Next spring, alas, both on this hillside and in the area at the ranch where we'd put the mulch, there was only a tiny showing of the evening primrose! Can you not get germination by the hay-mulch method? Was there not enough seed-soil contact? Or timely rain? What is the mystery? This is what I long to find out. If the desire becomes widespread enough to see certain roadsides, or your own driveway, or certain areas around your house covered with this lovely, early, drought-resistant plant, will we then learn how to get those tiny seeds out of those little pods? And if there is a market, will there be a supply? It allures me; it escapes me; I will try.

Pink evening primrose,
(Oenothera speciosa)
Texas. JOHN SHAW

Phlox and Blue Tradescantia

One spring day in 1985, I set out with a friend to look for wildflowers along the roadside, realizing that it was early in the season but hoping (because we had been able to steal the day) that we would find some flowers blooming. My companion was John Barr, a C.P.A., *and his passion is figures. But a love for wildflowers occurs in the most extraordinary of hearts, and he was one of our first National Wildflower Research Center dreamers and helpers.*

*It was on the road to Luling that we began to see along the right-of-way marvelous stands of Indian paintbrush (*Castilleja indivisa*) and also some good stands of bluebonnet (*Lupinus texensis*), the Texas state flower, not yet in full bloom. The first red-pink-purple phlox began to appear—thick stands of multishaded phlox (*Phlox drummondii*) among the bluebonnet and paintbrush. It intrigues me to think that phlox, so numerous it might well have been the state flower, was first taken as seed from Texas to England by a British explorer/botanist named Thomas Drummond in 1835. There it flourished in exquisite English gardens and was bred up to become an array of garden hybrids.*

*The Guadalupe River runs through the small city of Luling. It is a crystal-clear stream that winds between cypress trees, its banks lined with ferns—a beautiful piece of country south of Austin. There, right on the highway where a bridge crosses the river, stands a rusting cotton gin built to use the waterpower. We turned off the road and stopped, and there I caught my breath—for all along the banks underneath the cotton gin, beneath the tall trees, was a carpet of purple-blue flowers. They were tall—perhaps eighteen inches—with long foliage reminiscent of a lily. I recognized the plant as something we call by the unlovely name of spiderwort. It was a mass of tradescantia (*Tradescantia virginiana*)!*

There was a sign nearby, put up by the Texas Historical Association many years ago. Was it in the sixties when (in a brief period of nostalgia) we looked back and put historical markers on man's every effort to tame this wild Texas? The sign proclaimed that this was a gin built first to grind corn and wheat and later to gin cotton.

Spiderwort (*Tradescantia* sp.), Arizona.
CONNIE TOOPS

Red phlox (*Phlox drummondii*), Texas.
JIM BONES

Cotton-growing was one of those things man had attempted here that was not wise. The soil was too thin and not rich enough. Nevertheless, cotton was *produced in central Texas and the hill country for a brief twenty-year-or-so span—long enough to break a lot of pioneering entrepreneurs, among them Lyndon's father. This area is much more suited to feedcrops or cattle or sheep or goats. However, the gentle little valleys would indeed produce* some *cotton, just enough to keep up the hopes of man. Then came one of those depressions that occurred before the 1933 depression, and cotton fell from forty cents to eight cents a pound.*

I looked up across the road and gazed incredulously at the vast, blue stand of tradescantia spreading over what must have been a two-acre expanse in front of an old Victorian house. I looked greedily at the flowers and promised myself to find out from the tax collector whose land that was and if the landowner would let me come back to harvest seed for the Wildflower Center at the proper time. Why was tradescantia here in such profusion? Did man plant it at some time, and then did it spread, leaping the road, and go along the riverbank?

Spiderwort and paintbrush *(Castilleja* sp.*)*, Texas.
STEPHAN MYERS

Spiderwort, Florida.
MARGARETTE MEAD

To me it is wonderfully romantic, the spread of flowers. Somewhere in my reading, I discovered that a British naturalist named John Tradescant (both he and his father, also John, were landscapers and gardeners to King Charles I of England) had long, long ago made a trip to the New World, to record and collect various flowers that did not grow in England. Among them was this one, named by Linnaeus for the father.

I had seen spiderwort before, but never a field or carpet of it. Usually it occurs singly or in a small green colony. It grew on a granite outcropping that we once owned at the Sharnhorst ranch, a great knob of pink granite that rises above the surrounding pasture, a land of crags and huge rocks and fissures of quartz that run for yards along the rise. It is a wild, exciting place, where I loved to climb, around sunset, and sit down to look out across the world. There are little pools in which small minnows and frogs and fishlife swim—that is, if it has recently rained. If not, the pools dry up and are gone for months. And what happens with that life? And how do the creatures return when it rains? Growing out from under the rocks, where there must be only half-a-teacup of soil every now and then, there will be blue tradescantia.

Spiderwort *(Tradescantia ohiensis)*, Texas.
STEPHAN MYERS

I was told that in a park close to Gonzales, Palmetto State Park, there is some almost-tropical vegetation, one of those relic vegetation clusterings far away from its natural habitat. There one can find fields of tradescantia—purple-blue, pink, and white. I have never seen them. I had seen only individual plants that bloom in mostly damp places, until I found this field in Luling that fascinated me.

I wanted some seed of this tradescantia. Well, alas for plans. We were not able to find out the name of the people who owned the field. It had been rented, then sold. All our inquiries ended in confusion and put-off. A couple of months later, John drove back out to see if he could pursue the matter further, and, lo, some tidy and loving owner had mowed the field, clipped it flat, and it was covered with grass! Would the tradescantia come again? Would they survive? I hope I will remember to go back sometime late in March or in April—the Lord being willing—and see for myself. Perhaps next time I'll be more determined and successful.

Right behind the Wildflower Center, there is a steep bank heavily shaded with trees that goes down to the Colorado River. The slope must be always rather moist, and I envision tradescantia growing there. I believe that we *won't cut them down!*

John Barr and I continued our stolen day, passing more and more fields—gorgeous carpets of mixed wildflowers. When I would see bluebonnet, paintbrush, phlox of many colors, and no big rocks in the field, I would greedily think that this would be a good field to mow for seed. Every now and then we would see a pasture, an abandoned field, that would be white with prickly poppy.

Prickly poppy *(Argemone polyanthemos),* Texas.
ROBERT P. CARR

*We came to an ancient bridge with wrought-iron work and timbers that clack-clacked as the car went over them, and we had arrived at the "Thomas–Barr Estate"—a 550-acre tract along the San Marcos River jokingly so called because Don Thomas and John Barr had bought it as a wild adventure in hopes that down the road a few years somebody would pay them more than what they paid. On the left, just as we were about to enter John's domain, my eyes were caught by a field of red buckeye (*Aesculus pavia*), a shrub I knew in deep East Texas. Here it was, 350 miles away from my home, its candelabra of bright-red blossoms taking me right back to my childhood! What qualities of the soil caused it to be here also? How did the seed come? All of this is a wild romance to me.*

We turned in at a gate, unmarked. By this time, we were wishing we had brought along some sandwiches and cold drinks, but neither of us could turn back to get them because we were both so thrilled at the expanses of flowers opening up before us.

Such concentrations, such palette-brush glory of yellow daisy, bluebonnet, paintbrush—many things I didn't recognize. And then, in the wooded areas, again there was phlox, multicolored. I remember that some people call them post oak pinks. The mesquite trees were not out yet, and most other trees were bare. Mesquites, it is said, know when winter is really over and don't come out until then. It's the same with pecan trees; they're the last to put on their green leaves.

We rode through the "estate" delirious with the thought of coming back three months from then and harvesting seed for the benefit of the Wildflower Center. Because nature is prodigal and will have dropped a few million seeds, it won't hurt anybody if we take a few million others.

Somewhere along the road to Gonzales, we passed an old ghost of a house with white columns, huge magnolias, and the traditional driveway lined with cedars of Lebanon. Once more, as in the case of the cotton gin, I had to wonder whose high hopes had built this house, and then what had happened to them.

We came to Palmetto State Park, but too late, too hungry to stop and explore—with time enough only to note the still-handsome stonework built in the 1930s by the Work Projects Administration and the National Youth Administration. A little farther on, we saw a pipeline right-of-way that looked like a colorful crayon mark drawn across the countryside: a sunny open space filled with a ribbon of wildflowers.

Prickly poppy, Texas.
JIM BONES

What Is a Wildflower?

Chicory *(Chichorium intybus)*, Connecticut. LES LINE

Monarch butterfly on goldenrod *(Solidago* sp.*)*, Connecticut. LES LINE

Common roadside chicory *(Cichorium intybus)*. From Leonhart Fuchs, *De Historia Stirpium*, Basel, 1542. ROBERT RUBIC

The literal definition of a wildflower is simply "the flower of a plant not in cultivation." There simplicity ends. Our own experiences and prejudices, where we live, romantic allusion, biology, history, and a host of other factors shape our individual reactions to the term *wildflower*. The old axiom that one man's orchid is another man's weed is nowhere more true than in the interpretations of what a wildflower is.

A weed is a plant out of place. While Queen-Anne's lace and chicory may be beautiful along a road, they may not be acceptable in a rose garden, where, according to individual evaluation, they may be considered out of place. Even given evidence that in England goldenrods are prized garden plants, no amount of coaxing, exposure to, or experience with this plant would ever succeed in convincing most Americans that they are anything but weeds.

Except for horticultural hybrids, clones, and man-made cultivated varieties (cultivars), all flowering plants are or have been wildflowers somewhere. Tulips, native to Turkey and ancient Persia, were first brought into gardens there, then transported to Europe, and eventually hybridized to give us the great array available today. The Empress Josephine of France gathered together wild roses from many parts of the world to plant at Malmaison; from these, modern hybrids were developed. The cardinal flower of the eastern United States, many species of Lewisia from the Pacific Northwest, mariposa lilies from the Southwest, and phlox, native throughout America in many species, are prized horticultural subjects in Europe and in other parts of the world having conditions suitable for their growth and flowering, or where such conditions can be simulated in a greenhouse. Yet they are wildflowers in the place of their origin.

Many of us think of wildflowers as delicate, ephemeral plants that appear from season to season and then disappear. This concept limits the term almost exclusively to herbaceous annuals, biennials, and perennials. Annuals complete their life cycle from

New England aster *(Aster novae-angliae),* Michigan. LARRY WEST

Bitter root *(Lewisia rediviva),* Montana. TOM AND PAT LEESON

seed-germination to seed-bearing in one growing season. Biennials require two growing seasons to complete their cycle: the seed germinates the first year and produces a basic rosette of foliage that survives the winter; the plant blooms the second year. Perennials are longer-lived plants that die back to ground level at the end of the growing season; new growth emerges from the same roots the following season. Corn-poppy (*Papaver rhoeas*) and bachelor's button (*Centaurea cyanus*) are annuals; wild carrot (*Daucus carota*) and common evening primrose (*Oenothera biennis*) are examples of biennials; New England aster (*Aster novae-angliae*) and the many goldenrods (*Solidago* spp.) are long-lived perennials. Some perennials survive for many years, others for just a few. The terms *long-lived* and *short-lived* are commonly used in horticultural and botanical designations for perennials. And since distinct lines tend to be drawn by human analysis rather than biology, there are plants described by botanists and horticulturists as "biennial or short-lived perennial." This indicates natural ambivalence on the part of the plants (an example of ecotypic variation) or that not enough is known about these plants to establish a more accurate designation. These more-or-less "soft" plants (that is, herbaceous as opposed to woody) are often referred to by plant professionals as forbs, to distinguish them from grasses, which also are soft-tissued.

The term *native plant* adds additional confusion to the question "What is a wildflower?" The two terms overlap but are not synonymous. Native plants are those that have existed in particular landscapes for a very long time; ferns, horsetails, and skunk cabbage, for example, have existed through the ages. South American, Central American, and Mexican plants moved into the Southwest and up the California coast as missions were established and are termed camp-followers. It is considered unlikely that many species came to our Pacific Northwest from the Aleutian Islands, Alaska, or Siberia, although it is possible that a few may have come with the earliest ancestors of the American Indians. But this creates a dilemma. At what point in time must a plant be known to have existed to be considered native or indigenous? The question is moot; it could be argued endlessly.

While it may be of interest to be aware of the difference between indigenous and introduced wildflowers, the distinction has little to do with everyday enjoyment. For educational purposes, however, or when restoring a site to a particular era, the distinction becomes significant. The Native Plant Garden of the New York Botanical Garden, for example, is limited to plants indigenous within a 200-mile radius of its site in the Bronx. It does not contain any of the many introduced wildflowers that are evident along the edges of nearby roadsides, in highway interchanges, parks, vacant lots, and even within the confines of the overall Botanical Garden. The purpose of the Native Plant Garden is to help students and visitors to the garden understand the difference between indigenous and introduced.

The distinction is also critical when restoring a particular landscape, such as a prairie, or an American Indian encampment or village site to its original condition. Accuracy would require that the landscape simulate a time before the coming of the

Europeans, because most of the introduced wildflowers that are familiar today did not exist on this continent before European settlers arrived. Their impact on the landscape, particularly through the clearing of woodland, and the importation of seeds for gardens stimulated mass migrations of plants from Europe and brought about conspicuous changes in plant communities and the overall appearance of the land. The arrival of European settlers, therefore, makes a valid cutoff point for drawing the line between native and introduced plants. Of the unknown numbers of introductions, only those plants preadapted for North American conditions flourished.

The North American Indians, however, grew pumpkins, squashes, beans, and corn of Central and South American origin. While indigenous to the Western Hemisphere, these plants are not indigenous to what is now the United States and cannot sustain themselves. They can be grown only with direct human intervention, so the line drawn at the arrival of Europeans has, after all, a certain ambiguity about it.

Nor can we suppose that the introduction of foreign plants to our landscape and their naturalization began and ended in some remote historical time. It is an ongoing process that can be beneficial or destructive, depending on how specific kinds of plants behave in particular environments and how we manage those environments.

The wildflowers of the present-day United States, therefore, are a great mixture and amalgamation of species from practically everywhere else on earth with our own native plants, some of which are the most beautiful in the world.

Queen Anne's lace *(Daucus carota),* Connecticut. LES LINE

Blue phlox *(Phlox divaricata),* Connecticut. LES LINE

Evening primrose *(Oenothera biennis),* Michigan. LARRY WEST

Native Plants

Great lobelia *(Lobelia siphilitica),* Michigan.
JOHN SHAW

The continental United States, exclusive of Alaska and Hawaii, reaches, from east to west, about one sixth of the distance around the Northern Hemisphere and about the same portion of the distance from the North Pole to the equator; it is a large country. Elevations range from nearly 300 feet below sea level in Death Valley to above 14,495 feet at Mount Whitney. Annual precipitation is over 100 inches in some parts of the Pacific Northwest, less than 5 inches in the Sonoran and Mojave deserts. Soils vary from acid to alkaline, from rich and humusy to thin and poor. Precipitation can be in the form of rain, snow, or sleet, but some plants depend only on coastal or mountain mists. Not only does the number of sunshine days vary from place to place each year but the sunshine varies in intensity according to atmospheric conditions and solar angle. To speak of native plants and wildflowers, then, is not to speak about a neatly defined entity but, rather, a complex combination of biological units, colonies, or populations, each of which inhabits particular sets of conditions referred to as "ecological niches."

Where and how our native wildflowers originated is a question that is unanswered. Fossil remains reveal evidence and indicate the origins of some species living today. Many of today's plants are very old, some surprisingly young. Through mutation and natural hybridization over long periods of time, new species arise. Through study of fossil pollen grains and chromosomes with their component genes it is possible to identify the mass of genetic diversity available to create new species. From this information we gain insight into how new species of plants come to exist.

How New Wildflowers Originate

While hybridization of horticultural plants is achieved through manipulation by humans and, within limits, is predictable, the process in the wild is complex. If pollination takes place between two different species and viable seed are produced, success is still seldom assured. Some hybrids are weak or, mulelike, may be unable to reproduce themselves. In other cases, hidden physiological defects may prevent seedlings from growing to maturity and bearing seed. If the line is to continue, hybrids must be able to produce plants like themselves and be enough unlike either parent, genetically, so they will not backcross with one of the parent species. The basic key to understanding the creation of a new species through hybridization is that the plant that results from the cross-pollination of two different species must be able to produce plants like itself that, in turn, will produce plants like themselves. Most crosses of horticultural plants, for example, give rise to an array of variations, and this generation, in turn, produces offspring similar to its parents, to the grandparents, and some unlike any forebears. None of these would constitute a new species. In horticulture, desirable variants from among this array of hybrid offspring are propagated asexually (stem, leaf, or root cuttings, or by tissue culture), thus avoiding sexual (pollination-seed) reproduction and the recombination of genes that would result.

The Spiderwort: Evolution Revealed

A dramatic example of the gradual evolution of a new species is recounted by Edgar Anderson in his book *Plants, Man and Life,* 1952. In his study of the familiar garden spiderwort, long accepted as *Tradescantia virginiana,* he found that such was not so. Linnaeus, the Swedish botanist who established the present-day method of plant nomenclature, had named the plant in honor of John Tradescant, credited for first growing the plant in England.

During the 1920s, germ plasm of *Tradescantia* was studied with the goal of establishing some general principles of evolution. The conflicting theories that arose captured Dr. Anderson's imagination; thence began an odyssey that took on qualities of a detective story and lasted for years.

The crux of the results is that the *Tradescantia virginiana* that has been growing in English gardens (including botanical gardens, where it continued to be so labeled) is unlike the *T. virginiana* growing wild in Pennsylvania and westward to Missouri and south into East Texas. After Dr. Anderson had collected this and other spiderworts and had studied spiderworts throughout the length and breadth of their ranges, the clue came from his own garden, where two other species, *T. ohiensis* and *T. pilosa,* were growing near each other. The first, called railroad-track spiderwort, is a plant of open spaces. The latter, a plant of deep, shaded woodlands, was so unlike familiar spiderworts that Dr. Anderson had difficulty recognizing it. While they occur near each other over thousands of square miles of the Midwest, their ecological niches are distinct, so they did not have the opportunity to hybridize until brought into his garden and in close proximity to each other.

From this chance event Dr. Anderson proved that the Virginia spiderwort of English gardens was not the true *Tradescantia virginiana* as labeled but a hybrid between itself and the two other species that did not grow near it in the wild; in gardens all three species grew side by side. The change was so gradual and took so long (300 years?) that the transition from the original plants to a new and slowly evolved species went unnoticed. This new species, capable of reproducing itself without offspring that resemble their three ancestors, now carries the name *Tradescantia Xandersoniana* in recognition of Dr. Edgar Anderson and his work. Here is evolution visible, but made possible by human intervention: the movement of plants separated in the wild into gardens where they grew close together and were afforded the opportunity to create a new species.

From this illustration comes yet another lesson. It suggests that strong natural forces, such as floods, tornadoes, hurricanes, avalanches, and typhoons, can cause dramatic movement of plants, particularly of seeds, to new sites where they may come into associations where new opportunities for hybridization and the gradual evolution into new species can occur.

Spiderwort seems bound to man forever; it was discovered that spiderwort is an indicator of human exposure to radiation.

Pilose spiderwort (*Tradescantia pilosa,* now *T. subaspera*). First sent to Glasgow Botanic Garden by Thomas Drummond in 1833, this spiderwort is one of the species included in *Tradescantia X andersoniana.* From Curtis, *The Botanical Magazine,* London (vol. 61, plate 3291), 1834.
ROBERT RUBIC

The true *Tradescantia virginiana* as included in the Anderson research. From Redouté, *Le Liliaciae* (folio 2, plate 75), 1805.
ROBERT RUBIC

Spiderwort *(Tradescantia ohiensis),* Michigan. ROBERT P. CARR

Early goldenrod *(Solidago juncea),* Connecticut. LES LINE

Cardinal flower *(Lobelia cardinalis),* Michigan. LARRY WEST

Great lobelia *(Lobelia siphilitica),* Michigan. JOHN SHAW

In the case of Dr. Anderson's spiderworts, it was demonstrated that, in the wild, the plants did not hybridize simply because they did not grow close enough to each other for the pollen to travel from one species to the other. But distance is not the only factor involved, as was demonstrated by A. B. Stout, the man responsible for initiating the breeding of daylilies. Dr. Stout had growing in his garden two familiar native wildflowers: cardinal flower (*Lobelia cardinalis*) and great blue lobelia (*L. siphilitica*). He wondered, since the plants are closely associated in their natural habitats, why he had never seen any indication of hybridization between the two. To attempt such a cross, he fastened together two flower stalks that were growing side by side and removed some of the upper florets of the cardinal flower; the result simulated a spike with red flowers at the base and blue ones at the top. He then observed that bumblebees, responsible for the pollination of lobelia, would start at the bottom of the spike and work their way upward, carrying the ripe pollen from the lower flowers to the newly opened upper ones, but when they got to the blue flowers, they became confused and refused to continue their upward journey. No matter how many bees came to this spike or how often a single bee returned, none proceeded upward to the blue flowers after having visited the red ones below. These observations led to the recognition that, for some plants at least, bees (and possibly other insects) do not go from one species to another. Some of this may be due to color or preference for certain nectars, some because of a substance in the plant they find repelling; maybe a slight structural variation in the flower discourages or prevents such visitation; or maybe the plant may have evolved to attract specific kinds of insects but not others. The processes of the natural world are complex; it is not surprising that natural hybridization is an uncommon occurrence. If it were easily achieved, the world of plants might be chaotic; the system has its built-in methods of control through complex relationships involving other forms of life as well.

Modern-day laboratory equipment such as the scanning electron microscope and other, ever-more advanced techniques make it possible to study plant chromosomes and tissues to a finer degree than heretofore. Such knowledge reveals ever-greater differences and raises the dilemma of just where to draw lines of distinction between one species and another. Goldenrod provides an example of such a dilemma. One kind (*Solidago canadensis*) is treated by a leading authority as a transcontinental species having several regional varieties. To another authority, each variety is a distinct species. Plant taxonomists (classifiers) are "lumpers" and "splitters," but it is well to keep in mind the fact that plants are biological; humans, intellectual. Plants often reveal biological gradation, hence are not always easily classifiable. Compared to the cardinal flower and the great blue lobelia the species of goldenrod are so many, so diverse, so widespread, and often so similar to each other that they represent a complex and confusing group. The wild asters, relatives of goldenrod, also constitute a large and confusing group. Both reveal the incredible resources of plants not only for survival but for evolution through hybridization.

The Adaptable Pre-Columbian Sunflowers

The genus to which sunflower belongs, *Helianthus,* suggests evolution by hybridization assisted, perhaps, by the intervention of the American Indians. Totaling about 150 species of herbaceous annuals and perennials that appear throughout the United States, they are adapted to a wide variety of habitats, including wetlands, woodlands, arid and grassland areas, fertile humusy soils, trash heaps, wastelands such as roadside drainage ditches, and land along railway tracks. Until herbicides came into use, it was a common sight to see Midwest railroad yards completely blanketed with sunflowers; as if they had adapted to the situation, they flowered low enough to be unharmed by the trains. Wherever humans have gone, sunflowers have followed. The sunflower is the consummate American plant: tenacious, brash, bright, open, varied, optimistic, and cheerful, it might well be considered the true American flower.

Sunflowers had a long association with humans in pre-Columbian America; they are plants of antiquity. Carbon dating establishes the existence of sunflowers over 1,500 years ago in several parts of the United States. They were important to Native Americans long before corn and beans were brought from Central and South America. The sunflower is also the only plant originating in what is now the continental United States that is of world importance as an economic plant. The sunflower is the source of vegetable oil for much of Asia, where it is used as a salad oil, a cooking oil, in the canning of fish, and in feed for livestock; the oil also serves as a carrier for pigments in paint, and the stalks are used for fuel. In North America, Indians used sunflower seed for food, ground into meal and flour, and for oil. They selected different types of plants for oil content, the quality of flour or meal that could be made, and the seed quality itself, an indication of their high degree of agricultural sophistication.

Lewis and Clark, during their 1803–1806 expedition, found sunflowers plentiful among the Shoshone Indians, and an abundance of other evidence, both observed and archaeological, attests to the importance of this plant not only as food but for dyes and medicinal remedies and in religious ceremony. As a symbol, the sunflower merges with the sun in sacred and decorative motifs.

The first published description and illustration of the sunflower appears in Dodonaeus (or Dodoens), *Historie des plantes,* 1557. Sunflowers attracted attention throughout Europe and soon appeared in gardens everywhere. Nicholas Monardes, in *Joyfull Newes out of the Newe Founde Worlde,* 1577, wrote of "The Hearbe of the Sunne":

> This is a notable hearbe, and although that now they sent mee the seede of it, yet some yeres past wee have had it here, it is a straunge flower, for it casteth out the greatest flowers, and the moste perticulars that ever hath been seen, for it is greater then a greate Platter or Dishe, the whiche hath divers coulers. It is needefull that it leane to some thyng, where it groweth, or elles it will bee alwaies falling: The seede of it is like to the seedes of a Mellon, sumwhat greater, his flower doth tourne it selfe continually towardes the Sunne, and for this they call it of his name, the whiche many other flowers and hearbes do the like, it showeth marveilous faire in Gardines.

The "greate dishe" is, indeed, just that. What is commonly considered the "flower" of this plant is really a flower head or disk bearing hundreds of small, individual flowers. Each seed is the ovary, before pollination, of its own minute flower complete with stamens, anthers, and pistils in a tiny cuplike arrangement of petal tissue. The large "petals" at the outer rim of the flower head are not petals in the usual sense but, instead, are each the fused petals of a single, sterile "ray" flower. The function of this showy "ruff" seems to be to attract bees to pollinate the flowers of the disk.

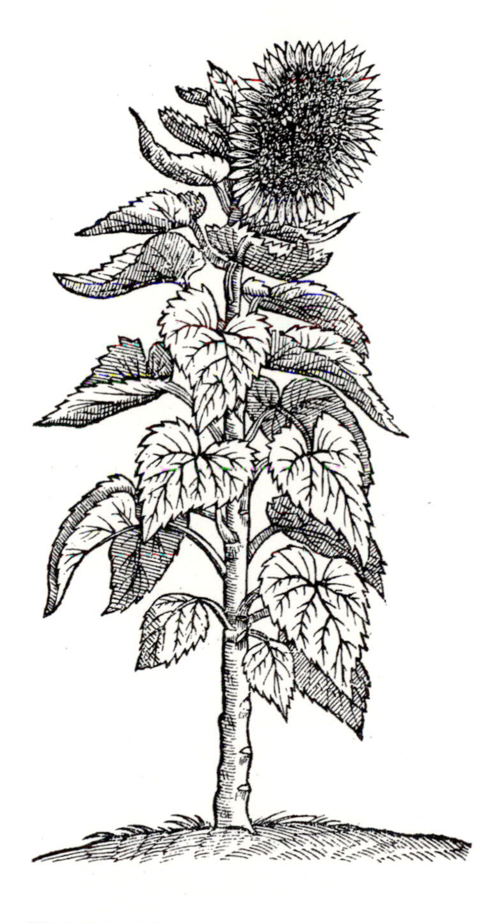

Considered to be the first published illustration of sunflower *(Helianthus annuus),* this woodcut was copied by Gerard in his *Herball* (1597) and by many others in later works. From Reinbert Dodoens, *A Niewe Herball or Historie of Plantes,* 1578.
ROBERT RUBIC

(Overleaf)
Field of cultivated sunflowers (*Helianthus annuus*), Wisconsin.
RUSS KINNE

This great flower head has another quality: it really does face the sun and follow its movement through the day. It is no romantic notion of poets. Dr. Edgar Anderson says of the sunflower head, "As soon as the ray flowers are conspicuous and before any of the [disk] flowers have actually opened, it faces the sun early each morning and turns slowly with it all during the day. Before sunrise the next morning it will still be facing the west but by half an hour later it will have swung back to the east. This movement is repeated day after day until the head is nearly through flowering and is heavy with developing seeds." As Erasmus Darwin noted in *The Botanic Garden: A Poem in Two Parts,* 1807,

Great Helianthus guides o'er twilight plains
In gay solemnity his Dervise-trains;
Marshall'd in *fives* each gaudy band proceeds,
Each gaudy band a plumed Lady leads;
With zealous step he climbs the upland lawn,
And bows in homage to the rising dawn;
Imbibes with eagle eye the golden ray,
And watches, as it moves, the orb of day.

The impressive physiological characteristics of the sunflower and its very long association with mankind are worthy of a lifetime of study. Indeed, several botanists, ethnobotanists, archaeologists, and other scientists have done so. We may well wonder how much the evolution of this plant is man-related. We may well wonder about its first beginnings. But this is true: From its complex natural history, its persistence, its great appeal as a symbol of the sun, and its usefulness, we gain insight not only about this plant but the plant kingdom as a whole.

Seeds of yellow salsify
(Tragopogon dubius),
Colorado. LES LINE

How Plants Migrate

While introduced plants are transported and distributed by humans, mostly through agriculture, the distribution of native plants depended, at least originally, on natural forces. Windborne seed is the most efficient means of distribution. Dust-fine seed can be carried for miles; seeds with parachutelike attachments (dandelion, milkweed) only fractions of miles; and those with winglike attachments (maple) only a few yards. But year after year even those yards can expand the range, provided the seeds find conditions suited to germination and growth. It is easy to visualize offspring of a particular tree growing only a few feet away from the outer reach of its branches, and then the offspring of this second generation growing beyond their parents. Eventually a whole grove might become established and remain centered on the site of the original tree. But if growing conditions were better at the lower edges of a hillside site, the whole grove would attain a new center as offspring at the lower levels grew and reproduced in greater numbers and reached maturity earlier than those on the uphill side, where fewer seeds would germinate and those that did would produce trees of diminished vigor. While a tree or a grove of trees is not mobile in itself, it would, in effect, have migrated down the hill over a period of generations.

The same effect is possible with plants having underground rhizomes, or "runners." Soil conditions influence the numbers and direction in which they grow. As the underground stems send up new shoots, new plants are established, which, in turn, develop more rhizomes. Obviously this is a

Seeds of common milkweed *(Asclepias syriaca),* Connecticut.
LES LINE

Fruit of red maple *(Acer rubrum),* Connecticut.
LES LINE

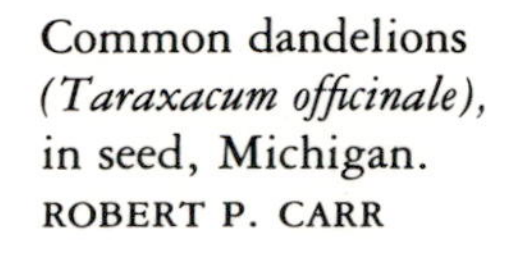

Common dandelions *(Taraxacum officinale),* in seed, Michigan. ROBERT P. CARR

more rapid method of migration than the tree example. Distances are limited by the length to which the underground stems can grow each year, but over a long period many perennial wildflowers (forbs) are able to create large colonies from what started as a single seedling. While a milkweed seed with its parachute may travel much greater distances, its problems are that it cannot sail upwind and that the seed may land in a place unsuitable for growth. The rhizomes, or underground stems, of aster or goldenrod, however, can reach out to take advantage of better soil conditions. Indeed, they, too, may migrate in much the same manner as a grove of trees.

Burrs, "stick-tights," and "hold-fasts" are seeds that have barbs and hooks; they stick to the coats of animals and to clothing. When a dog comes home with clusters of burrs under his ears, he is demonstrating how these seed are designed to travel. Bison, antelope, mountain goats, and hosts of other animals have been vehicles for what must have been billions of seeds over the centuries. In addition, mud clinging to their hooves carried more seed. Even the mud clinging to the feet of aquatic birds carries seed of shoreline and marsh plants and is considered by many naturalists the most efficient method of distribution for such plants.

Rainwater running along the surface of the ground, ocean currents (for shoreline plants), floods, the digestive systems of mammals and birds: All have contributed to the migration of wildflowers, sometimes over vast distances.

Common burdock *(Arctium minus),* Connecticut. LES LINE

New England aster *(Aster novae-angliae)* and goldenrod *(Solidago* sp.*),* New York. LES LINE

Great Discoveries

By the seventeenth century, when Europeans arrived on the North American continent, the evolution and migration of wildflowers had been going on for many millennia with relatively little disturbance. Although agriculture was practiced by the American Indians, who also gathered food and medicinal and other useful plants, their influence on wild plants was, so far as we know, minimal. Certainly it cannot be compared to what happened after the coming of Europeans. They first came to exploit the land, to take what they could from it, and they hoped to find a shortcut route to the riches of the Orient. They dreamed of gold but harvested lumber instead. The great white pine trees of New England were marked with the Crown and became shipmasts for His Majesty's Navy. The Europeans' gardens consisted of a few plants, the roots and seed of which they had brought with them, but from local Indians they soon learned to grow corn, pumpkins, and various squashes.

The seventeenth and eighteenth centuries were also the time of the great herbalists, and the search for new curative plants was intensified by the promise of a vast new continent to explore. The herbalists, too, learned from the Indians, as indicated in the specific name Linnaeus gave to the great blue lobelia (*L. siphilitica*). So zealous was the search for curative plants that goldenseal (*Hydrastis canadensis*), sassafras (*S. albidum*), sarsaparilla (*Aralia nudicaulis*), and ginseng (*Panax quinquefolius*) were gathered in shipload quantities for the European market. Medicine had moved from complex medieval concoctions to simpler, more direct remedies.

Great lobelia *(Lobelia siphilitica)*, Wisconsin. LES LINE

Leaf of sassafras *(Sassafras albidum)*, Michigan. LES LINE

Introductions

The European migrations brought thousands of wildflowers to North America. Many are considered weeds—and there can be no doubt that some are—but since beauty is in the eye of the beholder there is little need to worry about such a distinction.

Wildflowers came with the Spanish to Florida, Mexico, and eventually California; they came with the French to Canada, the Great Lakes, and down our interior rivers; and they came with the English, Dutch, Germans, and Scandinavians who settled the Atlantic seaboard and moved westward. As time passed more people came, and with them came plants of all kinds. Some were brought by intent; some came as hobos using whatever form of transport was available to them. The weedier and less conspicuous ones never became more than tramps; few became aristocrats. The great appeal of most of these immigrant wildflowers is their very commonness; they are available everywhere to everyone.

This mass movement of people brought about a mass movement of plants. Some came as weeds in agricultural crop seeds; others in cereals and grains; in packing materials such as straw and hay; in ship's ballast; in pants cuffs, in seams, and in other articles and parts of clothing; in soil clinging to boots and shoes; and in household goods and supplies. Others were brought as herbs for flavorings, dyes, scents, and medicinal remedies, and some very few came as garden ornamentals. Many of these plants found new homes for themselves by escaping from gardens and cultivated fields, and spreading beyond wagon trails and roadsides to become so widely distributed that they are now assumed to be native plants. Eastern meadows in June abound with such familiar plants as ox-eye daisy, buttercup, hawkweed, and several kinds of clover and other legumes brought from Europe as grazing and fodder plants, along with bluegrass, timothy, redtop, and other grasses; California coastal areas and hillsides are covered with wild-oats, fennel, and wild-radish; these plants so dominate the landscape that even a knowledgeable botanist might find it difficult to find an indigenous pre-Columbian plant among them. Although not native, these and other Old World plants have become so much a part of the American landscape that to visualize it without them is nearly impossible.

Most conspicuous in numbers are the immigrants that inhabit the eastern portion of the United States and extend westward across the Mississippi to the Great Plains. There are several reasons for this: the major movement of people was from the East Coast westward across the continent; after initial exploitation and large-scale clearing of eastern forestlands, the easy-to-till grasslands to the west stimulated a formidable movement of settlers and of agricultural seeds, supplies, and equipment; the movement from east to west was long-enduring; the introductions, immigrants, and escapes from gardens of Old World origin found growing conditions in eastern and midwestern America similar to those of Europe, including not only soils, rainfall, temperature, and other

Orange hawkweed *(Hieracium aurantiacum),* New Brunswick.
LES LINE

Ox-eye daisy *(Chrysanthemum leucanthemum),* Wisconsin.
R. HAMILTON SMITH

Red clover *(Trifolium pratense),* Connecticut.
LES LINE

Hawkweed *(Hieracium* sp.*),* New Brunswick. LES LINE

Common buttercup *(Ranunculus acris),* Connecticut. LES LINE

climatic similarities but also cleared land under cultivation. Continuing disturbance of the soil by plowing, harrowing, planting, harvesting, grazing, and mowing created ideal conditions for seed to germinate and plants to become established because it eliminated competition of more aggressive species. On whatever scale practiced—the vast corn acreage of the Midwest and Great Plains, California missions, or home gardens—agriculture provided opportunities for nearly universal distribution and establishment of European plants. Where nonnative wildflowers grow, therefore, is linked closely to climatic conditions that influence agriculture, whereas the distribution of native plants is more closely related to natural vegetative regions that existed long before European settlement.

Old Plant, Old World

The term *Old World* is commonly used in horticulture and botany to describe a plant from Europe–Asia, yet the more we dig into the relationships of some of these plants the more the term takes on another meaning: that some are very old plants, indeed. They have been around for a very long time, and their associations with man, too, are ancient.

A plant very closely linked to agriculture through very many centuries is the familiar but handsome narrow-leaved plantain, or rib-grass (*Plantago lanceolata*). A Danish botanist, Johannes Iverson, found pollen grains of ancient origin by boring into peat bogs. None was evident until the first agriculturists arrived in Neolithic times. "At this point," writes Edgar Anderson, "there

Narrow-leaf or English plantain *(Plantago lanceolata)* has been associated with mankind since neolithic times. From Leonhart Fuchs, *De Historia Stirpium,* Basel, 1542. ROBERT RUBIC

Common plantain *(Plantago major)* has followed the footsteps of man from northern Europe and Asia to many others parts of the world. The American Indian sometimes referred to it as "white man's foot." From Leonhart Fuchs, *De Historia Stirpium,* Basel, 1542. ROBERT RUBIC

is sometimes a narrow band of charcoal in the peat, showing that the land must have been cleared by fire. Just above the charcoal, pollen of such woodland plants as ivy disappears completely for a time, whereas rib-grass, previously unknown, becomes abundant and increases progressively, layer by layer." Where this plant came from originally is open to question, but the fact of its association with agriculture indicates that it was transported by man, however unintentionally, to broad regions of the earth where agriculture has existed. It is also interesting that its broad-leaved relative, the English plantain (*Plantago major*), is called cart-track plant in some parts of the world. While vernacular names are of little use in identifying plants in an orderly fashion, often, as in this case, they reveal or suggest past associations with people. The soil in cart tracks may be compacted enough to prevent other plants from growing but is not detrimental to this plant. Rainwater gathers in cart tracks, so more is available than in other places, and the seed may have been deposited with mud stuck to wagon wheel rims. An ecological niche may come into existence because of the action of man, and there seems always to be a plant to fill a special situation no matter how it may have come about. The American Indians called this same plant white-man's-foot, a name that echoes cart-track plant ecology and origin.

Old Plant, New World

The common tawny daylily (*Hemerocallis fulva*) is closely identified with the western movement from Europe to the Atlantic coast and onward across America. It is thought to have been brought to Europe from China by Marco Polo or by Phoenician traders. In China the flower buds were eaten both fresh and pickled, and the foliage was useful for feeding livestock. (Deer, the new suburban scourge in much of the United States, seem to relish it in early spring.) From the Mediterranean the plant traveled northward through Europe and to England. The English, in turn, brought it to New England and Virginia; later it was carried to the middle colonies by the Dutch, Germans, Scandinavians, and others. Eventually it was loaded into Conestoga wagons and carried westward; by then its food value had long been forgotten.

Tradition has it that where wagons were abandoned or burned, or loads had to be lightened along the Oregon Trail, the daylilies survived and hence came to be called ditch lilies. Another vernacular name reveals a less romantic facet of this plant's use in the farmsteads of the Midwest: privy plant. It also is called tiger lily, but it is not a true lily and should not be referred to as such; thus the prefix *day* should always be used in referring to this plant (otherwise, hemerocallis).

Because this daylily is sterile and does not produce seeds, the only means of dispersal is through the rootstock of the plant. Since it had little economic importance, it was carried around the world simply because it was attractive, bright, and reminded people, in new lands, of home.

Much like humans, the plant introductions, immigrants, and escapes came from the Old World and somehow, somewhere, found homes for themselves in the new.

Daylily *(Hemerocallis fulva)*, Connecticut. LES LINE

Purple loosestrife *(Lythrum salicaria),* Connecticut. LES LINE

Aggressive Introductions

The introduction of aggressive plants that have the potential to invade woodlands, grasslands, and wetlands to the detriment of existing ecosystems (ecological niches or conditions) in which plants and other organisms may be functionally altered or destroyed is an ever-present threat. Classic examples of such invasion are spiked or purple loosestrife (*Lythrum salicaria*), oriental bittersweet (*Celastrus orbiculatus*) and multiflora rose (*Rosa multiflora*), kudzu (*Pueraria lobata*), Japanese honeysuckle (*Lonicera japonica*) and several shrubby loniceras, and wild oats (*Avena sativa*). While on the surface these do not seem to be dangerous plants—after all, it is a beautiful sight in late summer to see acres of wetland colored magenta pink with loosestrife, or the bright orange-red of oriental bittersweet hanging in great masses from trees in autumn, or the multiflora rose both in flower and in autumn fruit—these plants not only crowd out native species but radically change the environment that sustains them.

The Strife of Purple Loosestrife

Possibly the most destructive of the herbaceous wildflower invaders is spiked or purple loosestrife (*Lythrum salicaria*). While there are loosestrifes of gardens that are not invasive (*L. virgatum,* for example, upon which several cultivars are based, has escaped only locally in New England), spiked loosestrife has invaded both salt-water and freshwater marshes and other wet places. It arrived from the Old World probably before 1831, the date reported in the first herbarium sheet (Ronald L. Stuckey, *Bartonia,* vol. 47, 1980). It may have arrived in ballast. Since it is not illogical to assume that soils used for ballast came from ground bordering harbors, it is easy to visualize how this wetland plant got aboard ships that crossed the Atlantic. When the ballast soils were removed in American ports to make room for bulky return cargoes of timber, cotton, and tobacco, they no doubt were dumped in the nearest convenient place at the water's edge or in a marsh near the harbor of arrival.

It is difficult, however, not to admit that this plant is beautiful; many square miles of marsh and damp roadside turn brilliant magenta pink in late summer throughout the greater Northeast and parts of the Midwest. It has spread from Nova Scotia and New Brunswick to the Dakotas and appears sporadically in Colorado, Utah, Washington, Oregon, and California. Southward it appears in the Carolinas, Oklahoma, and northern Texas. The tragedy is that this plant so completely takes over wetlands that it has eliminated many of the sedges, grasses, and other plants upon which marsh birds and animals depend for food. In addition, while technically it is a herbaceous perennial that starts new growth from the crown at ground level each spring, the flower stems of the previous year are so tough that they do not fall and decay during the winter, as is the case with most herbaceous perennials. Even when the plants are in bloom in late summer, the previous year's flower stalks remain upright. During the winter the thicket of persistent stems catches wind-blown leaves and other plant residue, and when the stems finally do fall they are slow to decay and fill in the wet places, which allows shrub and tree seeds to germinate and grow. Wetland sedges, rushes, grasses, and other plants are forced out. Although other plant and animal life eventually will move into this new environment, waterfowl and other forms of aquatic life that depend on wetland are displaced. While this is a natural process, it is the acceleration of the process by purple loosestrife that overwhelms associated native flora and fauna. On a small scale this situation could be considered just another example of succession of landscape from one phase to another, but so intensive and rapid is the invasion of this plant that in one area of New York State, where only a few of these plants were observed in 1951, more than a thousand acres had become infested by 1979. So serious is this invasion that a Purple Loosestrife Task Force has been organized in the state of Wisconsin, and other conservation organizations in other states are trying to find methods to selectively eradicate this plant in places where it is unwanted.

The Bitter in Oriental Bittersweet

Oriental bittersweet (*Celastrus orbiculatus*), through its climbing habit, is capable of destroying its host tree. The leafy canopy reduces the quantity of direct sunlight reaching the tree, thus diminishing its vigor. Furthermore, as the twining stems of the vine increase in girth, a strangulation

Oriental bittersweet *(Celastrus orbiculatus),* Connecticut. LES LINE (See also page 57)

effect develops and the conducting tissues beneath the naturally expanding bark of the tree become restricted. The weakened condition of the tree, combined with the sheer weight of the vine, eventually may cause the tree to fall to the ground. The bittersweet is rarely killed by the collapse of its initial host; with the resultant additional light penetration, it is able to grow with even greater vigor. In this example it is necessary to recognize that oriental bittersweet is in a foreign environment and that most of the natural predators (animals, insects, disease organisms) of its home environment are not here to keep it in check. American bittersweet (*Celastrus scandens*), which does not behave in this manner, is a somewhat smaller and less vigorous plant, partly because it serves as host to other organisms of its native habitat.

In general, it is the lack of natural predators—mice, moles, voles, reptiles, and other small animals, grazing mammals, birds, and particularly insects and disease organisms—that allows plants to grow out of control in a foreign environment. It is precisely this factor, conversely, that makes it possible to grow sunflowers as an economic crop in Asia; in the United States, the numerous competing organisms that have evolved with the sunflower (and with each other) make it impossible to grow the sunflower profitably after the second or third year on a given site. So interwoven is the mesh of ecology that to destroy even an invisible thread is to risk an unraveling. Fortunately the system has sometimes surprising energy for adjustment and repair, but today's intensifying onslaughts are so far beyond those of any other time in plant and human history that we may be on the brink of annihilation. And our willful ignorance is abysmal.

Edwin Way Teale writes about standing at the crest of the Continental Divide in *Journey into Summer,* 1960. "As we stood discussing such things (as the joy of the spot), two businessmen struck up an acquaintance nearby. They talked endlessly, loudly, always on the same subject: the clubs they had belonged to. . . . All the while the great spiritual experience of the mountains was passing them by. Unseen, unfelt, unappreciated, the beauty of the land unfolded around them. The clubs of the world formed their world entire. It enclosed them like the home of a snail wherever they went. For them, the scene would have been just as moving if they had been hemmed in by billboards."

Multiflora rose *(Rosa multiflora)*, Ohio.
GEORGE LAYCOCK

A Rose That Is Not

The manner in which we use land has profound ecological impact in aiding and abetting the spread of potentially harmful plants. Multiflora rose, for example, has invaded what were farmlands. In the 1930s Louis Bromfield touted and vigorously promoted the use of this rose for hedgerow barriers to grazing animals, and for protective cover and winter food for small animals and birds. The fields of his Malabar Farm, near Mansfield, Ohio, were bounded with this rose, and thousands of other conservation-minded landowners took up the challenge by planting thousands of miles of other fence rows with this plant. But what went wrong? As long as the farmlands were grazed by livestock or were cultivated to grow crops, the seed-bearing fruits and their seedlings were eaten or physically destroyed and were unable to grow to maturity. But once the farms went out of production and grazing animals were removed from the land, multiflora rose was no longer kept at bay. It took over open farm fields so completely that it is now impossible to make one's way through the extremely dense and thorny thickets of this rose. The very birds that were thus provided with winter food, deposited the seed, through their digestive tracts, across vast areas so that the plant now grows along roadsides, in parks, suburban lots, and wetlands, and even in lightly shaded woodlands. So densely do these plants cover and shade the ground in open places that other plants have little opportunity to penetrate the thick canopy. This is but one of several examples of a plant introduced to this country for seemingly good reasons, worthwhile goals, and practical needs that became disastrous. It must be recognized that socioeconomic factors have played a role in this evolution: the loss of the great dairy herds and the disappearance of farms in the East created conditions advantageous to the conversion of multiflora rose from a useful wildlife habitat and hedge to a noxious weed. And we are yet to find out what the longer-term ecological effect will be. As more and more farmers give up the land, this process portends unhappy ecological results for the future.

Marston Bates, in *The Forest and the Sea,* 1960, wrote, "It looks as though, as a part of nature, we have become a disease of nature—perhaps a fatal disease. And when the host dies, so does the pathogen. . . . I think we must make every effort to maintain

Common mullein, flannel plant *(Verbascum thapsus)*. From Leonhart Fuchs, *De Historia Stirpium,* Basel, 1542.
ROBERT RUBIC

diversity—that we must make this effort even though it requires constant compromise with apparent immediate needs." Thoughtful and knowledgeable management of agricultural lands going out of production today could prevent dustbowl conditions and other serious problems in the future. By seeding native grasses and forbs it is possible to return the landscape to at least a semblance of its natural, stable, and self-sustaining condition until needed again for production. We could, in a sense, give the country back to the country.

While a number of herbaceous wildflowers have the potential to become invasive, particularly on disturbed sites where construction or erosion have removed topsoil, they usually do so for only short periods. In the long run they may help to repair landscape because, through succeeding generations, they add organic matter that improves soil and allows other plants to grow on the site. For example, such plants as Queen-Anne's lace, yarrow, and mullein may dominate a site to the exclusion of other plants for a year or two, but unless conditions are extreme, they are not apt to do so for many seasons. A field that may be a solid mass one year may have but a few plants of the same species the following year. Evidence of the ability of some plants to withstand the harsh conditions of disturbed sites is seen in their abundance along roadways, where they inhabit hard-packed berms and are exposed to salt, gases, and other pollutants. Each species has its role, either by taking advantange of a site where competitors cannot survive or by being a link in the chain of succession to other plants. The concept of "invasiveness," then, is also a matter of scale. It ranges from something so widely spread and detrimental as spiked or purple loosestrife to relatively small areas (a few acres, a field, the corner of a garden) and disturbed soil situations where plants are part of the healing process or provide cover where other plants will not grow. In general, plant invaders should be evaluated on the basis of their function in a particular landscape at a particular point in time. It is important to recognize the negative aspects of loosestrife, multiflora rose, oriental bittersweet, and other such damaging plants and, when necessary, to initiate eradication procedures. But it is also important to recognize that other plants, even the introductions, immigrants, and escapes, may be functioning in more subtle, long-term processes that, in the end, can be beneficial.

Common mullein *(Verbascum thapsus)*, Michigan. LES LINE

In popular parlance and to landscape-oriented individuals throughout most of the United States, the term *wildflower* generally refers to herbaceous annuals, biennials, and perennials. Collectively they are widespread (although individual species often are narrowly endemic or show restricted ecological amplitude, and they therefore provide enormous challenge). They are within the scope of most horticultural techniques, offer great diversity, and can be selected for compatibility with existing geographical and ecological situations. They also are ever-changing (in no two years is a planting or site exactly alike) and, barring the introduction of an aggressively invasive species, are not apt to lead to landscape damage, destruction, or disaster. Errors can be avoided and corrected through the understanding and use of biological, ecological, and horticultural techniques.

Out of the Past: Observers and Enthusiasts

Modern-Day Explorers

Discovering Indian Pictographs

Indian blanket *(Gaillardia pulchella)*, Texas. DAVID MUENCH

Indian blanket, Texas. LARRY WEST

One of the happiest things that can befall us is to love the land we live in! One day my daughter Lynda and I were off to the Catto Ranch near Alpine, Texas, to see Indian pictographs—early drawings on cave walls in the arid Amistad area of West Texas. It was November 1965, and my friend Nancy Negley had suggested this outing. Mr. Jack Catto, a lean, spare man with a white mustache and a very genial manner, met us at the airport, along with his foreman Travis Roberts, who looked as if he never could have fitted into anything but western clothes. Leather-skinned and craggy-faced, he was straight out of the earth of West Texas.

We drove about an hour to the Catto Ranch, to a small, unpretentious house, bright on the inside with Mexican paintings, rugs, and bowls, and old artifacts of the country. A little swimming pool was on the terrace outside, which looked up to a grand view of the mountains.

We picked up Mrs. Catto, who was carrying a great basket with a picnic lunch, and started out in their car. And then we began the most interesting six hours. Just what I like most! West Texas was new to me. We drove through a dry valley full

*of staghorn-cholla cactus (*Opuntia imbricata*) with what I first thought were yellow blossoms. They turned out to be multitudes of persistent fruit and seed. The soil was bone dry and the vegetation sparse—the land looked like what might have been left over when the world was made. There were a few mesquite trees, desert below, and suddenly, behind one tree, a huge black-tailed deer, a buck almost twice as large as the white-tailed kind we have in central Texas. The long ears of this species have earned it the name mule deer.*

This is a country beloved by archaeologists and geologists. Parties from all the universities come in the summer on field trips. (It was on such a field trip at the Catto Ranch that one group, over a period of several months, unearthed a dinosaur skeleton and carted if off without notifying the obliging landowners, who had given them permission to explore; then their school asked the Cattos if they would like to pay for a building to house the dinosaur!)

As we approached the mountains, it appeared we were going to run right into them, but then we entered a cleft aptly called Doubtful Canyon. The road, which wound along the floor of the canyon, is sometimes transformed into a streambed after a rain. On each side of the canyon the walls tower to the most marvelous formations. One wall, right in front of us, was similar to the entrance of a cathedral, carved and dramatically standing forth like the masterpiece of some giant race of architects.

Tree cholla *(Opuntia imbricata)*, New Mexico.
ROBERT P. CARR

The Cattos pointed out "the doughnut hole"—a perfect hole so many feet above us that it seemed small, though it was probably six feet across. The most delightful thing of all was the brilliant blue sky, the bright sunshine, and the utter sense of being the only people who had ever found Doubtful Canyon. Now the streambed was quite dry, but there was some vegetation here—walnut trees, yellow with the touch of fall, and some white oak. Then we saw a great many Mexican piñons—small, picturesque, perfect Christmas trees. Travis Roberts asked, "Would you like to see the rock where the Indians used to sharpen their tools?" We did, indeed.

We walked a ways toward an overhanging ledge, and there was an enormous, round rock scarred with wedges made by long-dead Indians. How long ago—hundreds or is it thousands of years?—had they sharpened their spears and axes by drawing them back and forth across the stone, finally wearing troughs or slits? On the ground below the rock were countless pieces of flint, broken bits of their tools. It practically *spoke* to us, this rock. You could hear where the big axes went, and also the small spear points. Our hosts were full of stories about this country.

Later we saw another overhanging ledge in the distance. We made our way over the canyon floor, strewn with boulders, and here it was that I saw my first madrona tree, a beautiful specimen—the trunk crooked and ashy white before the bark flakes off to a dull red—very picturesque and loaded with bright red berries. Against that sparkling blue sky it was a breathtaking sight! Just beyond the ledge we found the Indian pictographs, the work of a rather primitive, unsophisticated tribe. They used red, black, and a sort of mustard yellow color. Their drawings were geometric, simple designs. The floor and overhang of the ledge were black with smoke. Charles Tunnell, the archaeologist who accompanied us, said the Indians had probably used this as a shelter, and the blackened ledge was the result of years and years of cooking fires.

By now we were getting hungry, so we found a place on the valley floor, which was covered with white pebbles smoothed by many years of flowing water and shaded by walnut trees, and set out our picnic table. Never have I enjoyed a meal more! After lunch, we found our most interesting Indian pictograph, quite a way in, possibly a mile from the cars, over very rough terrain. We walked almost straight up, or so it seemed. When you looked back you saw innumerable madrona trees, all bursting with red berries. We clambered around huge boulders and finally up so steep an ascent that I *knew I would be frightened if I looked back. Finally we were on a narrow ledge, hugging the cliff, with a big overhang that protected it from the weather.*

Here, for the length of about two city blocks, drawings lined the wall. One of the most fascinating may have been a calendar. It was possibly thirty feet long, with little cross marks at rather regular intervals. Again the colors were red, yellow ocher, and black. And these Indians were somewhat more sophisticated than the others. With a little imagination you could make out stick men. There were dozens, hundreds of them. We took pictures. We felt like discoverers!

All the time that we had been climbing, the staghorn-cholla cacti we'd seen in the valley below were giving way steadily to piñon and madrona trees, particularly along the beds of little streams. Finally we saw a stand of maple, its foliage still brilliant crimson and scarlet, but a little past its prime. It excites me to think why maples should be there, so far from their ordinary habitat. By now we had reached about 5,800 feet, and at this high altitude there was abundant grass, thick and knee high. The view was magnificent. We were within sight of the Big Bend country and the Chisos Mountains. But by all odds, once more, the most delightful part was feeling we were the only people who had ever been there!

Many had, of course—the Apache and Comanche, and a scattering of ranchers. And, interestingly enough, it was close to here, about the time of the Civil War, that an army lieutenant had led a camel expedition across Texas, trying to see if camels would make good draft animals for the army in this part of the world.

As we descended into Chalk Valley, there were lots of mule deer and some of my old friends the white-tailed deer, just like the ones at home. We saw a covey of blue-headed quail, dozens of them—large birds, with bright blue heads, that ran along the ground before they flushed. Then, for the first time, I saw a coyote in the wild! He was really a rather bedraggled-looking animal—a small, lean, brown dog with a bad disposition running swiftly away from us. And, to crown it all, we sighted a herd of antelope! They, too, were far away and very swift, their snow white rumps bounding away across the floor of the valley.

Tired and happy we bid our hosts farewell. It was a day of wonderful adventure for Lynda and me—our own sort of day—archaeology, exploring, being together.

Gathering Seed of Bluebell and Mountain Pink

Mountain pink
(*Centaurium beyrichii*)
PAUL M. MONTGOMERY

Do you ever think of lost opportunities? One of those I remember is when I got a frantic call from a lady near Houston who told me in rising decibels that close to her home there was a field of bluebell—about a fifteen-acre field—that the farmer who owned it was going to plow up the next day and put in oats. Could I come and get them, harvest them, dig them up, save them, buy the land? I couldn't. I wasn't swift enough, inventive enough, aggressive enough. But the thought lingers in my mind—one of those things I wish I had done.

I recall the first time I ever saw a vast field of bluebells. It was a day of high adventure during the White House years on one of our visits back to Texas. In the morning, I went with Dr. and Mrs. Donovan Correll, both outstanding botanists, in search of flower seeds. It all began when I saw some bluebells in a church at Johnson City. I had tracked them down as coming from a neighboring ranch.

Dressed in blue jeans and boots, I set out on this carefree expedition, but soon had to turn back and get the owner, Mrs. Gibson, for a guide. She had known Lyndon all his life. She wore a sunbonnet and had that delightful combination of dignity, friendliness, and simplicity that I fondly, and probably quite wrongly, imagine to be possessed mostly by country people. She was glad to drive us over to the field to see the bluebells. Yes, they had been blooming all summer—a vast sheet of blue. We went south through the pastures—lovely pastures dotted with large live oaks—gradually climbing 'til Johnson City was in the valley below us. Finally, we emerged on a wide, grassy meadow in full sunshine. The land was moist and rich, and there were hundreds on hundreds of bluebells still in bloom, though they had been at their peak, Mrs. Gibson said, two weeks or a month before. Dr. Correll identified them as a member of the gentian family, Eustoma grandiflorum.

(Overleaf)
Mountain pink
(*Centaurium beyrichii*)
Texas.
PAUL M. MONTGOMERY

He was excited, got out and took pictures, and said that never before had he seen so many bluebells in all his searching across Texas for wildflowers. With his thumbnail, he cut open one of the seed pods, and it was still wet and sticky and green. You could see the dozens of tiny seeds that in time, when they were dry, might possibly

Mountain pink *(Centaurium beyrichii)* Texas. PAUL M. MONTGOMERY

be germinated by spreading them out in some meadow. We tried to pick a few. Consensus was that they simply were not ready. Mrs. Gibson said we could come back anytime and get all we wanted—there is such a generosity of spirit in people here. We were having a marvelous time. The sun was beating down and the day getting on. Since we couldn't gather seed, we took Mrs. Gibson home and left for the Diamond X Ranch.

*I had talked to Nita Winters, and she had told me we could come out and pick as many mountain pinks as we wanted. Mountain pink (*Centaurium beyrichii*) is like a little nosegay of tiny pink flowerets—hundreds of them—completely covering the strawlike stem so that the plant looks like a dainty pink powder puff. They grew in the most incredibly barren caliche soil on a hillside strewn with rocks. They were past blooming now—just little globes of pure straw, with here and there a pink blossom. Dr. Correll thought they must have dropped millions of seeds where they were, so when we saw a hillside offering a few plants we got out and walked and found more and more and more. From each we took half of the little globe of flowerets, leaving the rest for Nita's hillside to make sure that prodigal nature was left with some of its abundance. We stuffed our trophies into envelopes until three of them were bulging. And then, hot, successful, and happy, we headed back to Johnson City, stopping at Lyndon's boyhood home long enough to have some cool lemonade with Jessie Hunter and look at the grounds, which really were in very good shape.*

Dr. and Mrs. Corrrell told me about some of their adventures when he had been part of a botanical team in search of a plant that produced cortisone. Cortisone had just been discovered then, and it was a good hunch that it occurred naturally in a plant. He told me about other plants he had found and isolated that were toxic to livestock; naturally ranchers wanted to identify and eliminate them.

After lunch, near a curving road, I put out my few bluebell seeds. Along the LBJ Ranch runway, an impossibly barren stretch of caliche, we crumbled up and let fly the tiny bouquets of mountain pinks. Twenty years later, there are a few clumps of flowers to speak of that day.

And then back to the main house, where Dr. Correll showed me some of the plants he had picked, pressed, and preserved between sheets of paper—thousands upon thousands over the years. And "somewhere through it all," I wrote in my diary that August day, "runs a thread of purpose."

Plant Explorers of the Past

There may be in this world no souls more generous than those of plant explorers, be they Scotsmen, Englishmen, Germans, Swedes, Frenchmen, or Spaniards: the fascination of the New World bred feverish enthusiasm that carried them through earthquakes, floods, Indian wars, famine, boat-swamping rapids, mosquitoes, infections and disease, searing heat, and penetrating cold in the search for new plants. And their patrons at home—royalty, nobility, scholars, nurserymen and seed merchants, or professional or landowner gardeners smitten with the same passion—lived their days in excited expectation of each new shipment, of each new root, bulb, or cutting, and the germination of each new seed not only from North America but from Asia and Australia, Australasia, South America, Africa, and the tropical isles of the Pacific. Such names as Tradescant, Bartram, Catesby, Banister, Linnaeus, Kalm, Hooker, Drummond, Michaux, Lewis and Clark, and Douglas are forever bound to the history of plants through plant nomenclature. Genus designations such as *Clarkia, Tradescantia, Lewisia,* and *Kalmia* and the specific epithets *drummondii, douglasii,* and *michauxii* are familiar to serious gardeners, foresters, conservationists, and botanists everywhere.

Many of the plants indigenous to what is now the continental United States were collected and sent to Europe (especially to England) during the seventeenth century until "by 1750 North America was the most significant source area with respect to the number of species available" (P. J. Jarvis, "North American Plants and Horticultural Innovation in England, 1550–1700," *Geographical Review,* October 1973).

The swift rise of interest in and acceptance of North American plants in England coincided with a period of rapid transition in English horticulture. From earliest times, gardens had been resources for practical needs. The orchard provided fruit; the kitchen garden provided roots, stems, leaves, and other table foods; and the herb garden was a source of necessary flavorings,

Swamp rose *(Rosa palustris),* Connecticut.
LES LINE

Wild pine
(Tillandsia polystachia)
by Mark Catesby. From
Natural History of Carolina, Florida and the Bahama Islands. London
(vol. 2, plate 89),
1731–43.
ROBERT RUBIC

medicinal remedies, scents, and dyes. Ornamental plants as such were not a part of these gardens.

But by the end of the reign of Elizabeth I (1558–1603), gardens had become elaborate with parterres, mazes, and knots and, according to Jarvis, "had a greater variety of plants and a greater complexity of patterns than their predecessors had, and [so called] *wild gardens* were carefully planted, often using newly discovered ornamentals." Under Oliver Cromwell (1649–58) the Commonwealth disapproved of and discouraged the cultivation of ornamental plants. It was during this period, however, that John Parkinson's *Paradisi in Sole Paradisus Terrestris* (1629) and Francis Bacon's essay "On Gardens" (1625) became widely read and accepted. Parkinson's was the first book to deal with ornamentals as such, and Bacon presented an idealized view of what a garden should be. By the time the Stuarts were restored to the throne (1660), providing a release from Puritanism, interest in ornamental plants was high. It is no wonder that so much effort was expended in the search for new plants in the New World and not surprising that they so rapidly became a part of English gardens.

By far the greatest effort to find new plants came from Great Britain. During the Revolutionary War, of course, Royalists were not welcomed in America, and again during the War of 1812, but by then such a collector as the Quaker John Bartram, who was born and lived all his life on the banks of the Schuylkill in Philadelphia, was able to maintain his collections. Plant collectors from England, on occasion, ran into difficulties with the French and the Spanish at the edges of their territories. Just as the Louisiana Purchase opened the West for homesteading, it opened vast new regions to the plant explorers, who ignored even the gold they walked on in streambeds so singleminded were they in their quests.

Nicholas Monardes, and Hariot and White

Before the northern Europeans began their explorations with such intensity, however, the Spanish had been to Florida, to the mouth of the Mississippi River, and to Mexico and California; evidence of their interest in plants of the New World is revealed by the writings of Nicholas Monardes (1493–1588) about sunflower and tobacco published in Spain and translated into English in 1577 under the title *The Three Books of Monardes or Joyfull Newes out of the Newe Founde Worlde,* and in a book published in 1615 by this physician to Philip II that contains information on many herbs under their Mexican names. And what of the Vikings? Who knows what natural prizes they took home from North America?

The first attempt at settlement by the British did not come until Roanoke Island in 1585, but the effort was doomed, largely because those who made up the group were more inclined to soldiering than agriculture. Fortunately, amidst this less than admirable group, there were two interested and observant individuals: Thomas Hariot, a mathematician and astronomer, and John White (fl. 1540–1590), who was adept at sketching what he observed and had the curiosity of a naturalist. The two men ventured to the

Bee-balm *(Monarda fistulosa)* was named in honor of Nicholas Monardes, physician to Philip II of Spain. From Curtis, *The Botanical Magazine,* London (vol. 5, plate 145), 1791. ROBERT RUBIC

Sea or marsh pink *(Sabatia stellaris).* Watercolor by John White, considered the first illustrator of American plants and a member of the Lost Colony, Roanoke, c. 1590. Reproduced by courtesy of the Trustees of the British Museum.

mainland to collect plant and animal specimens, which they took with them, along with written accounts and drawings, when they returned to England in 1586. (Thomas Hariot, *A Briefe and True Report of the Newfoundland of Virginia Diligentlye Collected and Drawne by John White,* 1590.) Some of the plants are described in Gerard's *Herball,* 1597. White's drawings, sometimes criticized for being possibly too much from his imagination (or embellished by others), recorded what Virginia was like in 1585. The two men observed, wrote about, and sketched Indian villages and gardens with melons, pumpkins, beans, squashes, and sunflowers. White made sketches of wildflowers, trees, fish and other animals, and other wildlife—altogether a remarkable record.

In 1587 White returned to Roanoke with more than a hundred men, women, and children, including his daughter and son-in-law, but the small company that had remained on the island had disappeared. Progress was made, however, but it was necessary for White to go again to England in a desperate attempt to get help for the Roanoke colony; when he returned in 1690 the inhabitants—including his daughter and granddaughter, Virginia Dare—had vanished. The only indication of their fate was carved on a tree: *croatoan;* had they been the victims of a nearby Indian tribe?

The Tradescants, Father and Son

The two John Tradescants, father and son, served as gardeners to Charles I. The senior John (?–1638), in 1611, traveled throughout the Low Countries and to Paris to purchase plants in his position as gardener to Lord Salisbury. He journeyed to Russia on a plant-hunting expedition in 1618 and to Spain in 1621. With his son, John II (1608–1662), he established the garden and natural history museum that came to be known as Tradescant's Ark. (The collections were later whisked off by, some think, a sly scientist named Ashmole, who was honored by Oxford in the name Ashmolean Museum of Art and Archaeology.)

Tradescant was a subscriber to the ill-fated Virginia Company and had great interest in America. In his list of 1634 are named some forty plants of American origin. In addition to growing trees and shrubs he is reputed to be the first in England to grow eastern columbine (*Aquilegia canadensis*), green-headed coneflower (*Rudbeckia laciniata*), *Aster tradescantii,* and, of course, the spiderwort (*Tradescantia virginiana*). While he himself did not visit America, his son, John II, came here in 1637, 1642, and 1654. Little is known of his collections except that the catalog of plants included in *Musaeum Tradescantinum* contains several American plants in addition to those listed in 1634, including red maple, tulip-tree, swamp cypress, and sycamore in addition to maidenhair fern, pearly everlasting (*Anaphalis margaritacea*), false Solomon's seal (*Smilacina racemosa*), lupine (*Lupinus perennis*), and a bergamot (*Monarda* sp.).

Perennial lupine *(Lupinus perennis),* an eastern relative of the Texas bluebonnet, was grown at the Oxford Botanic Garden as early as 1658. From Curtis, *The Botanical Magazine,* London (vol. 6, plate 202), 1792.
ROBERT RUBIC

Columbine *(Aquilegia canadensis)* was collected in Virginia by John Tradescant II. From Curtis, *The Botanical Magazine,* London (vol. 7, plate 246), 1793.
ROBERT RUBIC

Shooting star (*Dodecatheon meadia*). Mark Catesby, in his *Natural History of Carolina* . . . (1731–43) named this plant *Meadia* in honor of a Dr. Mead, but Linnaeus retained it only as a specific epithet. Shooting star is widespread; John Bradbury reports collecting it on the "prairie behind St. Louis." From Curtis, *The Botanical Magazine*, London (vol. 1, plate 12), 1787.
ROBERT RUBIC

John Banister and the Bishop of London

A prominent importer of American plants of the colonial period was Henry Compton, whose position as Bishop of London gave him access to many prominent people. He sent John Banister (1650–1692) to Virginia, where he arrived in 1678. An Oxford graduate, he was industrious and within two years had sent back a catalog of plants he had observed. It was published by John Ray in his *Historia Plantarum,* 1688, and is considered the first printed account of American flora. Banister's introductions—sent to the Oxford Botanic Garden, the bishop, and several correspondents—include familiar wildflowers: shooting star (*Dodecatheon meadia*), purple coneflower (*Echinacea purpurea*), and Virginia bluebell (*Mertensia virginiana*), in addition to sweet bay (*Magnolia virginiana*), and white swamp azalea (*Rhododendron viscosum*).

Dodecatheon is also credited to Tradescant and Catesby, but as plant-hunting activity increased in numbers of explorers and ever-expanding territory opened, it is no surprise that a given species of plant might be collected by more than one individual as new and heretofore unseen. The problems of preparing pressed, dried specimens, of keeping roots, cuttings, and seedlings alive, of keeping seed dry in torrential rains, swamped canoes, ocean storms, and even shipwreck, and away from mice, rats, and insects were daunting; that so much arrived in Europe is wondrous, indeed. In addition, while collectors predating Linnaeus (1707–1778) applied names to specimens, he later became the final authority with the publication of his *Species Plantarum* about 1730. Plants were received by Compton, Peter Collinson, and other correspondents and agents of American collectors, and they sent most of their dried herbarium specimens on to Linnaeus at Uppsala, Sweden. The time lag was long, but the names given sometimes recognized the collector, the correspondent, the sponsors, or the geographical locale from which a specimen came. Since Linnaeus had limited knowledge of North America and place names did not mean precisely what they do today, such specific epithets as *virginiana* and *novae angliae* did not mean Virginia and New England in today's terms, and *florida* simply means *flowering.*

Mark Catesby: Williamsburg's Audubon

Only the least observant of individuals could visit Colonial Williamsburg today without soon becoming aware of the presence of Mark Catesby (1679?–1749) in the form of reproductions of the bird plates of his *Natural History of Carolina, Georgia, Florida, and the Bahama Islands,* 1731–43. He had no scientific training and no financial backers in this undertaking. He simply sketched what he observed as he went along, then devoted the last twenty-three years of his life to producing the more than 200 plates and overseeing their publication.

> As I was not bred a Painter I hope some faults in Perspective, and other niceties, may be more readily excused: for I humbly conceive that Plants, and other Things done in a Flat, tho' exact manner, may serve the Purpose of Natural

History, better in some Measure, than in a more bold and Painter-like Way. In designing the Plants, I always did them while fresh and just gathered: and the Animals, particularly the Bird, I painted while alive (except a very few) and gave them their Gestures peculiar to every kind of Birds, and where it could be admitted, I have adapted the Birds to those Plants on which they fed, or have any relation to.

Because he included appropriate plants in his bird illustrations, he not only set the pattern for Audubon but recorded visually the flora of the areas he explored. In fact, many of his plates might better be considered plant illustrations with birds.

Catesby's sister lived in Williamsburg and was married to the prominent physician William Cocke, so it was not long before the talented naturalist met William Byrd II, who also had deep interest in the natural world. Catesby stayed in the Williamsburg area, venturing to the foothills of the Alleghenies, and gathered seed that he sent to Bishop Compton and Thomas Fairchild, a London nurseryman. By the time he arrived back in London in 1719, after seven years in America, his reputation had preceded him, so he was able to return to America under the sponsorship of a distinguished group of plant enthusiasts. He thereby became the first full-time professional collector of American plants. He arrived in Charleston in early May 1722, was received by the governor and local society, and then began his plant-hunting journeys. He visited plantations along the Ashley River, and traveled the Savannah River to Fort Moore, a frontier post he returned to twice so that he could observe the plants of the area at various seasons. After "exhausting the areas around Charleston" and attempting a trip to the Alleghenies, he went to the Bahamas; after spending a year collecting there, Catesby returned to England in 1726.

I was much delighted to see Nature differ in these Upper Parts, and to find here abundance of things not to be seen in the lower parts of the country. This encouraged me to take several Journeys with the *Indians* higher up the Rivers, towards the Mountains, which afforded not only a succession of new vegetable Appearances, but the most delightful Prospects imaginable, besides the Diversion of Hunting Buffaloes, Bears, Panthers, and other wild Beasts. In these Excursions I employed an *Indian* to carry my Box, in which, besides Paper and materials for painting, I put dry'd Specimens of Plants, Seeds, *&c.*—as I gather'd them. To the Hospitality and Assistance of these Friendly *Indians,* I am much indebted, for I not only subsisted on what they shot, but their First Care was to erect a bark hut, at the approach of rain to keep me and my Cargo from wet.

Mark Catesby's interest in plants was as much from the viewpoint of a gardener as that of a botanist-collector. As a result, many of his introductions include ornamental shrubs and trees, Carolina allspice (*Calycanthus*) and beauty-berry (*Callicarpa*) among them. He also introduced lance-leaf coreopsis, but while he sent many other plants to England, there were very few "firsts." His bird plates, however, are monument enough for any man. They continue to help us see not only the birds but the wildflowers he cherished so long ago.

Yellow lady's-slipper and black squirrel by Mark Catesby. He describes this orchid, "twelve to sixteen inches . . . yellow, hollow, of an oblong form, resembling an egg on the back part, tho on the fore-part open, having an apron or lappet hanging over the hollow," and applies the name *Petalis angustis* to it. This orchid is now known as *Cypripedium calceolus,* var. *pubescens.* From *Natural History of Carolina*..., London (vol. 2, plate 73), 1731–43. ROBERT RUBIC

John Bartram and Peter Collinson

Peter Collinson (1694–1768), a wool merchant and linen-draper of London, was not a botanist nor did he ever come to America; nevertheless, he was a major force in the history of exploration and importation of plants. Catesby considered him a cherished friend, but Collinson is probably better known for his relationship to John Bartram (1699–1777) of Philadelphia. Both were Quakers, and their correspondence is preserved in *Memorials of John Bartram and Humphry Marshall* by William Darlington, 1849. Bartram, a farmer, quite suddenly (and literally, as tradition has it) put down his plow, plucked a daisy and "viewed it with more curiosity than common country farmers are wont to do," and thus became a botanist. He began by studying Latin and was encouraged in his pursuit by like-minded people in Philadelphia who made their libraries available to him. From his farm he explored the Susquehanna and Allegheny rivers, Lake Ontario, the Shenandoah Valley between the Alleghenies and the Blue Ridge Mountains, and the Catskills. Southward he explored the coastal areas of Delaware, Maryland and Virginia, Georgia, and eventually, after Florida became a British colony in 1763, traveled upstream from Saint Augustine on Saint John's River. His energy and curiosity combined to make him probably one of the most productive of the botanist-collectors of the era, with an enthusiasm that continued to his death at the age of seventy-eight in 1777.

Marsh pink *(Sabatia grandiflora).* William Bartram wrote of this plant, in a letter dated September 6, 1810, "There are in the moist Savanas of Carolina and Florida many species of this charming plant, there called Savana Pinks." This is the same species as that painted by John White of Roanoke nearly two hundred years earlier (see p. 77). From *Fothergill Album: Drawings of William Bartram, 1756–1788,* The British Museum (Natural History). Published by the American Philosophical Society, Philadelphia, 1968. ROBERT RUBIC

Gerardia *(G. fasciculata,* now *Agalinis fasciculata).* Described and collected by Thomas Nuttall in 1818. He and William Bartram were enthusiastic about this plant of the rich savannahs. It grows six to eight feet high and its much-branched, slender stems are abundant with "many rose-colored flowers finely sprinkled with crimson specks." From *Fothergill Album: Drawings of William Bartram, 1756–1788,* The British Museum (Natural History). Published by the American Philosophical Society, Philadelphia, 1968. ROBERT RUBIC

John Bartram to P. Collinson.

September 30th, 1763.

Dear Peter:—

I have now travelled near thirty years through our provinces, and in some, twenty times in the same provinces, and yet never, as I remember, once found one single species in all after times, that I did not observe in my first journey through the same province. But many times I found that plant the first, which neither I nor any person could find after, which plants, I suppose, were destroyed by the cattle. . . . The first time I crossed the Shenandoah, I saw one or two plants, or rather stalk and seed, of the *Meadia,* on its bank. I jumped off, got the seed and brought it home, sent part to thee, and part I sowed myself; both which succeeded, and if I had not gone to that spot, perhaps it had been wholly lost to the world. John Clayton asked me where I found it. I described the very spot to him, but neither he nor any person from him could find it after. O! what a noble discovery I could have made on the banks of the Ohio and Mississippi, if I had gone down, and the Indians had been peaceably inclined, as I knew many plants that grew on its northeast branches. But we are at present all disappointed. My son William wanted to go as draughtsman.

I read lately, in our newspaper, of a noble and absolutely necessary scheme that was proposed in England, if it was practicable; that was, to search all the country of Canada and Louisiana for all natural productions, convenient situations for manufactories, and different soils, minerals, and vegetables. The last of which, I dare take upon myself, as I know more of the North American plants than any others.

Bartram's correspondence with Collinson, which began in 1730 and continued until the latter's death in 1768, is rich with details on collecting, transporting, and preserving specimens so that they could be studied by European botanists. Many of Bartram's collections were sent on to Linnaeus. Living in the days before the polyethylene bag, Collinson instructed Bartram to obtain an ox bladder whenever he came upon a farmer who had just slaughtered an animal. Small trees and shrubs, their roots dampened and inserted into the bladder (the neck of which was tied snugly closed around the plant stems), could then be hung from the pommel of a saddle or side of a cart. The plants remained in good condition until Bartram could plant them in his nursery in Philadelphia, which was considered the first botanic garden in America. Collinson also instructed him on building boxes: "make the bottom . . . full of large holes," and grow trees and shrubs in them for two or three seasons "till the plants have taken root and make good shoots," and then ship planter box and all to England. It also must have required great patience to get ship captains to cooperate by stowing plants in safe places for their passage. Excessive heat, cold, dampness, salt water, rats, and, not the least, a careless and uncooperative crew could negate years of work.

On August 12, 1737, Collinson writes, "Pray to send me the blossom and fruit of the Pawpaw in a little jar of rum. We never had yet a specimen of this tree in flower and I want much to see the fruit which will keep fresh in the rum. . . . Please to remember the Solomon's Seals that escaped thee last year." Collinson was demanding but generous in his concern for Bartram, sending him supplies, clothing, and books from time to time. He worked diligently to procure the position of king's botanist for Bartram. The appointment finally came in 1765 but with a pitiful annual stipend of £50. But Bartram's great contribution stands as his own memorial: the introduction of over 200 American species to Europe. While many explorers were more botanically than horticulturally inclined, Bartram had a good eye for beauty as well; it was said that he could not pass any plant that was beautiful. Among the herbaceous wildflowers for which he is credited are: trailing arbutus (*Epigaea repens*), black cohosh (*Cimicifuga raceosa*), dwarf crested iris (*Iris cristata*), several species of phlox, American turk's-cap lily (*Lilium michauxii*), wood lily (*L. philadelphicum*), beebalm (*Monarda didyma,* in honor of Nicholas Monardes), white hellebore (*Veratrum viride*), and a host of others. While Bartram's plant records were just that—records—he seems not to have kept a journal, and his good friend Peder Kalm bewailed the fact that "not a thousandth part" of the knowledge he had acquired did he put into writing. Such journals would have added immensely to information of the time. In part the revealing and glowing correspondence with Peter Collinson makes up for this lack. Whatever Bartram's faults, and Quakers seemed to try hard to have few, we cannot have anything but high respect for and feel warmly toward this unique individual.

John Bartram also traded in foreign plants. He procured peonies, oriental poppy, and other ornamentals from other parts of the world for clients in America, particularly for Thomas Lamboll of Charleston. For the introduction of Norway maple,

William Bartram's drawing contains American lotus or water chinquapin *(Nelumbo lutea),* Venus flytrap *(Dionaea muscipula),* and a great blue heron. It certainly displays Bartram's talent as an artist. From *Fothergill Album: Drawings of William Bartram, 1756–1788,* The British Museum (Natural History). Published by the American Philosophical Society, Philadelphia, 1968. ROBERT RUBIC

which he requested from Philip Miller of London in 1756 and soon thereafter offered for sale, we cannot admire him. But this is a small flaw. When Benjamin Franklin founded the Philosophical Society in 1743, the "common country farmer" became a charter member.

JOHN BARTRAM TO P. COLLINSON

May 1st, 1764.

Dear Peter:—

I have received my worthy friend's letter of January 1st, 1763, I suppose it should be '64. . . .

The broad-leaved Carolina *Commelyna,* and our narrow-leaved, is a late fall flower, and very different from the spring TRADESCANT'S Spider wort.

I had always, since ten years old, a great inclination to plants, and knew all that I once observed by sight, though not their proper names, having no person, nor books, to instruct me.

Peder Kalm of Kalmia

Peder Kalm (1715–1779), the son of a Finnish pastor, turned to botany and became a student of Linnaeus at Uppsala. He collected plants in Sweden, Finland, and Russia before being appointed professor of economics at the university at Abo. He was commissioned by Linnaeus to search for new plants and investigate the flora of North America in latitudes similar to those of Sweden. Linnaeus, who had been to Lapland, persisted with his concept that the tundra might be made productive if plant species could be found that would thrive there, and he assumed that the northern

Dwarf or crested iris *(Iris cristata),* sent by John Bartram to Peter Collinson in London and introduced by Collinson in 1756. From Curtis, *The Botanical Magazine,* London (vol. 12, plate 412), 1798.
ROBERT RUBIC

Turk's cap lily *(Lilium michauxii).* Introduced by Peter Collinson, via John Bartram, it was published here as *Lilium carolinianum.* From Curtis, *The Botanical Magazine,* London (vol. 49, plate 2280), 1822.
ROBERT RUBIC

reaches of the North American continent could be the source for such plants.

On the way to America, Kalm stopped in England to meet with Mark Catesby, Peter Collinson, Philip Miller, and others. Philadelphia had originally been colonized by Sweden, and many Swedes lived in the surrounding countryside and towns. After arriving, in the fall of 1748, along with a gardener named Lars Yungstroem, Kalm was deeply impressed with the fact that everywhere he looked he saw totally unfamiliar plants. He called on Benjamin Franklin, who made his library available to him, visited John Bartram, and remarks in his journal, *Travels in North America,* 1772, "We owe to him the knowledge of many rare plants which he first found and which were never known before. He has shown great judgment and attention which lets nothing escape unnoticed." That they became friends is not surprising. By the end of October, Kalm shipped a consignment of seeds and plants; it is obvious that he wasted no time in getting to work. In December he left Philadelphia to establish a base of operations in the Swedish village of Raccoon on the New Jersey side of the Delaware River; there he married a pastor's widow and eventually took her back to Sweden with him.

Kalm began his journey northward in May 1749. It was an arduous trip up the Hudson, Lake George, Lake Champlain, and overland to Montreal. From there he traveled down the Saint Lawrence. He made his way with the help of the governor of Quebec, who had received orders from France to assist Kalm, and from Quebec he made excursions northward. It evidently was a very uncomfortable experience, full of mosquitoes, ticks, blackflies, and gnats, and a forest so deep and dark that few plants were found. For some unexplained reason, Kalm's journals stop in early October, and details of further travels are not recorded in the same careful detail as the earlier ones, but he did succeed in sending home a consignment of seeds and other materials in late fall. In 1750 he followed the Mohawk River, through Iroquois territory, and explored along Lake Ontario and the Niagara Falls area. The following spring he sailed for Sweden, stopping again in England, where he saw flowers in bloom that had been grown from seed he collected in America. From Peder Kalm's collections Linnaeus described about 350 species in *Species Plantarum,* 1753. From Linnaeus came fitting tribute: one of the most beautiful evergreen shrubs of North America, the mountain laurel, he named *Kalmia latifolia.*

William Young, New Jersey Upstart

On December 5, 1766, John Bartram, seldom critical of others, wrote to Peter Collinson: "I am surprised that YOUNG is come back so soon. He cuts the greatest figure in town, struts along the streets, whistling, with his sword and gold lace, &c. He hath been three times to visit me—pretends a great respect for me. He is just going to winter in the Carolinas; saith there is three hundred pounds sterling annually settled upon him." Some individuals throughout history, botanists included, seem to succeed by loudness of trumpet or accident of birth. Whereas Peter Collinson worked for so long to gain for John Bartram

William Young, the "New Jersey Upstart," may have copied or adapted this watercolor drawing, *Nymphaea,* 1766–67, from previous illustrations by William Bartram and Mark Catesby. Botanically it is inaccurate and almost worthless. In terms of design, however, it suggests the Orient and Egypt. The Trustees of the British Museum (Natural History), London. Published in Ella M. Foshay, *Reflections of Nature, Flowers in America,* in association with the Whitney Museum of American Art. Alfred A. Knopf, New York, 1984. ROBERT RUBIC

the appointment as botanist to the king (and finally succeeded in 1765, when Bartram was sixty-seven years old), along came William Young (fl. 1740–1780) from New Jersey who, after a mere three years' experience as a nurseryman, was appointed botanist to the queen in 1764. He was the son of a farmer who was also representative for an English remedy called Hill's Balsam. John Hill, a manufacturer of herbal medicines, had less than a favorable reputation. Through his sponsor Lord Bute, Hill gained Young's appointment. Young went to London to study botany and returned two years later boasting of a salary of £300 a year. Compared to Bartram's £50, this seems not only unjust but reveals something of court politics. The queen of George III was German, and, the gossips had it, the Youngs were said to be of German descent.

Eventually Young redeemed himself by establishing a connection with Vilmorin, a plant and seed firm in Paris. In 1783 the firm published a list of American plants *par William Young, jr. Botaniste de Pensylvanie.* The list included 173 species of trees and shrubs, and 145 herbaceous plants that were available either as seed or plants. Young also sent plants to Kew and is credited with about twenty introductions. None became important as horticultural plants.

Michaux, André and François André

One of the great names of American plant exploration, especially to foresters and others particularly interested in woody plants, is that of the French botanist André Michaux (1746–1803). His was an official assignment. He arrived in New York with his son and a gardener in October 1785, where he made arrangements to send his collections to Abbé Nolin at Rambouillet and to the Jardin des Plantes in Paris. Instructed to establish a nursery where plants could be held for shipment at the proper stage of growth, he did so in New York and decided to establish a second one in Charleston, South Carolina, which has a longer growing season and a less severe winter.

Michaux explored the Savannah River, and retraced the trip of the Bartrams, John and his son William, up the Saint John River from Saint Augustine to Lake Saint George. Florida had been reclaimed by Spain; therefore he sent a collection of seeds to Madrid. When the French Revolution erupted Michaux expected to be recalled, but, instead, he was able to continue collecting. For the remainder of his stay in America he had no financial support from the French government, so, for income, he concentrated on the Charleston nursery, introducing ginkgo and silk tree (*Albizzia*), which he obtained from China traders. When able to, he resumed explorations, traveling northward to Montreal and Quebec. He proceeded up the Saguenay River to the trading post at Saint John and then continued northward into country unexplored by any European. Eventually the weather turned so cold that his guides refused to go on, so he found it necessary to turn back without reaching Hudson Bay.

The single-mindedness of Michaux next carried him westward, to explore Kentucky. Starting out in April 1795, he crossed the Cumberland Mountains to Knoxville, botanizing at every opportunity along the way.

From there he turned northward to Danville, Kentucky, and from Danville made two trips to Louisville, all the while traveling through the country occupied by dangerous Indians. He went on to Vincennes, Indiana, was injured in a fall from his horse, but in a few days continued collecting plants with the help of an Indian and his wife. Eventually he arrived at Fort Kaskaskia, on the Mississippi River, where he made his base. In December he started homeward, arriving in Charleston in the spring of 1796, a year after starting out.

The French Revolution financially ruined several plant collectors and other explorers who had been sent out by the government. Michaux had mortgaged his inheritance and had no choice but to return to France, to see what could be salvaged. The nursery in Charleston he could not sell because, technically, it belonged to the French government. Leaving the nursery in care of his son, he left for France in August with a large quantity of plants, seeds, and specimens. The ship, bound for Amsterdam, was blown off course and wrecked just off Holland. Michaux was unconscious when brought ashore. Personal belongings lost, his shipment was saved; he washed the salt water from the plants and spent six weeks drying out and remounting specimens. When he returned to Paris, he was received with honor but, except for a small portion of the salary due him, no award or income. He was assigned a piece of ground at Rambouillet for his collections, but little remained of the over fifty thousand trees and consignments of seeds he had sent home previously. Fortunately, some had been sent by Marie Antoinette to her father at Schönbrunn before she went to the guillotine, for Rambouillet was ruined.

The French government refused to allow Michaux to return to Charleston, so it was necessary for him to live frugally while preparing for publication his *Histoire des chênes de l'Amérique,* 1801, and *Flora boréali Américana,* 1803 (posthumous). He had accepted an offer to go with an expedition to Australia, but died of fever in Madagascar. His son, François-André (1770–1855), added to his father's legacy with his book *Histoire des arbres forestiers de Amérique,* 1810–13, the English translation of which appears under the title *North American Silva.* Although there has been criticism of some botanical details, all are significant works that not only helped foster better understanding of North American woody plants, in particular, but are landmarks in the history of botany and of American forestry.

Lewis and Clark

Probably no saga of American history has appealed more to adventurous imaginations than that of Lewis and Clark and their Northwest Passage. Despite the fact that neither Meriwether Lewis (1774–1809) nor William Clark (1770–1838) was a botanist, new botanical history was made by them. Both were veterans of frontier wars with Indians, both were expert woodsmen. In preparation for the trip, Lewis received instruction in natural history and Indian lore in Philadelphia, where many of his herbarium sheets and other specimens are in the Academy of Natural Sciences.

Fire pink *(Silene virginica).* One of the Michauxes (father or son) is credited with the introduction of this plant. From Curtis, *The Botanical Magazine,* London (vol. 61, plate 3342), 1834.
ROBERT RUBIC

Gigantic Erythronium *(E. giganteum,* now *E. grandiflorum),* in the same genus as the smaller and more familiar trout-lilies and adder's-tongue, is known as avalanche lily and was discovered by David Douglas in northern California. From Curtis, *The Botanical Magazine,* London (vol. 94, plate 5714), 1868.
ROBERT RUBIC

5714.
1.
2.
3.
W. Fitch, del. et lith.
Vincent Brooks, Day & Son, Imp.

The expedition had been organized but had to await the completion of the Louisiana Purchase by Thomas Jefferson. Immediately the well-equipped party of forty set off. Leaving Saint Louis in May 1804, the explorers worked their way up the Missouri River to camp near the Mandan Indians about fifty miles from what is now Bismarck, North Dakota. The following spring, 1805, they sent specimens back to Philadelphia before continuing westward. When they could no longer travel by water, they hired horses from the Indians and searched for places to cross the Rocky Mountains. Finally they arrived at the upper reaches of the Clearwater River in Idaho, built canoes, went downstream to the Snake River, entered the Columbia River near what is now Pasco, Washington, and, on October 7, they came to the Pacific. It was the first time the country had been crossed from east to west.

After spending the winter at Fort Clatsop near the Columbia River, they turned homeward, arriving in Saint Louis in September 1806.

In addition to making their collections of plants, mammals, reptiles, and aquatic specimens, Lewis and Clark had mapped and opened the West for the hundreds who were to follow. The forests and mountains of the interior and of the Pacific coast eventually would provide a whole new wealth of useful trees, garden ornamentals, and horticultural treasures. The collections of seed and plants and other specimens from the expedition consisted almost entirely of materials new to botanists, zoologists, and other scientists of the time. Although Osage orange (*Maclura pomifera*) is a much-heralded tree brought back from the trip, many choice herbaceous plants were discovered: several Clarkias and godetias (*Clarkia* spp.), blanket flower (*Gaillardia aristata*), a pink monkey flower (*Mimulus lewisii*), *Calochortus elegans,* the avalanche lily (*Erythronium grandiflorum*), and several Lewisias (*Lewisia* spp.). Both *Clarkia* and *Lewisia* were described and named in honor of the expedition's leaders by Frederick Pursh in his *Florae Americae Septentrionalis,* 1814.

Thomas Nuttall: Printer to Professor

A journeyman printer from Liverpool, Thomas Nuttall (1786–1859) arrived in Philadelphia in 1808. As a printer he was already interested in books, but an interest in plants led to Nuttall's meeting Professor Benjamin S. Barton (1786–1856) of the University of Pennsylvania, who soon became his friend, teacher, and patron. (Meriwether Lewis was instructed by Dr. Barton before his expedition to the Pacific; Barton also brought Nuttall and David Douglas together.) Dr. Barton was limited in physical ability, so he found in Nuttall someone who was not only observant and quick to learn, but someone who could do field collecting. Nuttall's first trips were to the coasts of Delaware and New Jersey and were financed out of his earnings as a printer, but Professor Barton planned more arduous collecting, for which he provided equipment and a monthly salary. The route was to take Nuttall to Winnipeg. (Barton's physical limitations did not stop him from making big plans, but he also may have been innocent of understanding the hardships involved.)

Early in 1810 Nuttall left Philadelphia for Pittsburgh by stagecoach; after that he traveled by boat or afoot.

April 22, 1810—In the afternoon I took a walk up the river *Monongahala*. The banks are high & steep, the shelving rocks were covered with *sedum ternatum, Phlox subulata Sanguinaria Can. Fumaria cucularia, &* the fine *Aconitum uncinatum* all in flower, the nectary of the Aconitum is small & not hooded, the spur of which is articulated & bent about the middle. flower, a fine Prussian blew below the rocks on the banks of the river, grew the *Viola Pensylvanica, Dentaria bulbifera,* a low pubescent species of *Phlox* stolonifera with large pale purple flowers & Pulmonaria Virginica with bright blue flowers. About 3 mls. up the river, nr. its banks, grew *Trillium* erectum now in flower, a *Tetradynamious* plant nearly in flower leaves trifoliate, & dentate; racema terminal, here were vast quantities of the Claytonia in flower, its leaves here were constantly lanceolate & obtuse, & nearly ½ an inch broad. I found resting upon the trunk of a tree a very large species of *caudated Sphynx* of a pale green color, its antennae were pectinated, or rather plumose; the wings rested horizontaly each wing was triangular; having 2 gems or eyes in each; it was nearly 2 inches aross the wings, the wings were edged with a pale crimson, the appendices or cauda were very long. After passing up the river about 5 or 6 mls. I crossed the river opposite a tavern & remained here for the night. ("Nuttalls Travels into the Old Northwest: An Unpublished 1810 Diary," in J. Graustein, ed., *Chronica Botanica,* 1951.)

Malaria was a constant problem for Nuttall, causing fever frequently, yet when no other way of getting to his destination was available—even water routes were not reliable because dry periods rendered boats useless—he walked.

May 24, 1810—To day I again betook myself to my unfortunate journey but I was very weak & unfit for what I had undertaken, the day was very warm, & I was uncommonly burthened having to carry the contents of my trunk upon my back & my gun in my hand thus situated I could make little progress. On my way I saw a species of *Asclepias,* which was new to me the leaves were in 4. verticillate, ovali-lanc. acuminate; rosaceous & odorous.

Not being able to get a boat for Detroit at Erie, Nuttall walked nearly 150 miles westward, as far as Sandusky, where he was able to get a boat.

June 10, 1810—To day I passed thro' a sandy plain covered with the ripe fruit of the *Fragaria,* & alive with snakes as the day was warm. I came to a small settlement on *Kiaoga* called *Cleveland* where I spent the remainder of the day. The *Lysimachia punctata* is here very abundant & near flowering, also *Galium latifolium* in flower the flower is of a brown-red—there is also a variety with whitish flowers; a species of *Phlox.* . . . It is just got into flower which is of a fine lake red, whilst the species I 1st met with at *Pitt.* is now generally in fruit, the flowers of this last species also were very odorous, but the species under observation is nearly inodorous, the leaf is somewhat fleshy the membrane on the under side of the leaf is very smooth & easily separated. I also met with a *species of convolvulus.* . . . The *Veratum luteum* is in flower in these sandy woods I also saw the *Frasera* nearly in flower, it seems quite a giant amongst herbaceous plants.

From Sandusky he traveled by canoe through Lake Huron but found himself unwelcome along the Canadian shores of Lake Superior, which were patrolled by the British and the North West Company. Michilimackinac was headquarters of the John Jacob Astor fur company, and Nuttall joined the Astorian Expedition that was planned to follow Lewis and Clark's path to the Pacific. En route, in Saint Louis, Nuttall met John Bradbury, who had been sent from Liverpool to look for new areas in which cotton could be grown and for new plants. Bradbury was sponsored by the Liverpool Botanic Garden and the Philosophical Society. Since both men came from the same part of England and both had a deep intertest in plants, they became friends. Nuttall succeeded in getting Bradbury to join the Astorian Expedition. They left Saint Louis with the expedition's leader in March 1811, planning to join the party near the mouth of the Nordway River and to stop at Fort Osage along the way. Nuttall made his headquarters at Fort Mandam, from whence he made many excursions, penetrating another hundred miles up the Missouri River.

Late in the year Nuttall returned to Saint Louis and New Orleans, where he was able to get a ship bound directly for England just before the outbreak of the War of 1812. He sent a large shipment to Professor Barton in Philadelphia and took seeds and plants to England. Many were contributed to the Liverpool Botanic Garden, some established in the garden of his uncle, and others marketed through a dealer in American plants. The botanic garden's 1813 catalog lists, among the herbaceous plants: Indian squill or wild hyacinth (*Camassia fraseri,* now *C. scilloides*), prairie coneflower (*Rudbeckia columnaris,* now *Ratibida columnifera*),

Opening white and fading to purplish-red, this is one of the showiest of the evening primroses *(Oenothera caespitosa)*, sometimes called matted evening primrose. It is believed to have been discovered by Thomas Nuttall. The evening primroses should not be confused with the spring-flowering garden primroses *(Primula* spp.*)* or any of the true roses (*Rosa* spp.). From Curtis, *The Botanical Magazine,* London (vol. 38, plate 1593), 1813. ROBERT RUBIC

tufted evening primrose (*Oenothera caespitosa*), and *Penstemon glaber*.

Thomas Nuttall returned to Philadelphia in 1815 to publish his *Genera of North American Plants,* 1818, and then left almost immediately for Pittsburgh, walking overland from Lancaster. He hired a boat to take him down the Ohio River, but because the Mississippi was too low to allow steamboat travel, he bought a flat-bottomed skiff, hired a boatman, and traded in flour, salt, and whisky as they went downriver. Along the shores he saw the destroyed and abandoned settlements resulting from the previous year's earthquakes and floods. At the mouth of the Arkansas River he turned upstream and arrived at Arkansas Post for the beginning of the spring season. In his journal he notes on January 21, 1819:

The path, which I this morning pursued to the Post, now town of Arkansas, passed through remarkably contrasted situations and soil. After leaving the small circumscribed and elevated portion of settled lands already noticed, and over which were scattered a number of aboriginal mounds, I entered upon an oak swamp, which, by the marks on the trees, appeared to be usually inundated, in the course of the summer, four to six feet by the back water of the river. . . . After crossing this horrid morass, a delightful tract of high ground again occurs, over which the floods had never yet prevailed; here the fields of the French settlers were already of a vivid green, and the birds were singing from every bush, more particularly the red bird (*Loxia cardinalis*), and the blue sparrow (*Motacilla sialis*). The ground appeared perfectly whitened with the *Alyssum bidentatum.* The *Viola bicolor,* the *Myosurus minimus* of Europe, (probably introduced by the French settlers) and the *Houstonia serpyllifolia* of Michaux, (H. *patens* of Mr. Elliot) with bright blue flowers, were also already in bloom. (R. G. Thwaites, *Early Western Travels, 1748–1846*, vol. XIII, "Nuttall's Travels into the Arkansa Territory, 1819," 1905.)

Continuing his river travels with a riverboat trader, Nuttall was able to collect plants whenever the trader went ashore to peddle wares at small settlements, some of only two or three families.

April 27, 1819—Yesterday I took a walk of about five miles up the banks of the Pottoe, and found my labour well repayed by the discovery of several new or undescribed plants. In this direction the surface of the ground is gently broken or undulated, and thinly scattered with trees, resembling almost in this respect a cultivated park. The whole expanse of forest, hill, and dale, was now richly enamelled with a profusion of beautiful and curious flowers; among the most conspicuous was the charming Daisy of America, of a delicate lilac colour, and altogether corresponding in general aspect with the European species; intermingled, appears a new species of *Collinsia,* a large-flowered *Tradescantia,* various species of *Phlox,* the *Verbena aubletia,* and the esculent *Scilla.*

Nuttall then traveled with troops, going overland to the Red River Valley:

May 22, 1819—The change of soil in the great Prairie of Red river now appeared obvious. It was here that I saw the first calcareous rock charged with shells, &c. since my departure from the banks of the Ohio. Nothing could at this season exceed the beauty of these plains, enamelled with such an uncommon variety of flowers of vivid tints, possessing all the brilliancy of tropical productions.

The plants included calliopsis (*Coreopsis tinctora*), white evening primrose (*Oenothera speciosa*), *Penstemon cobaea*, and *Rudbeckia maxima*. Dallying behind the troops to collect plants, he found himself alone, sought refuge with a friendly farmer for nearly a month, then joined a party of hunters and reached Fort Smith in June.

Nuttall then proceeded, with an agent of the boat-trader, to the Verdigris River in Oklahoma; the Neosho River in Missouri, Oklahoma, and Kansas; and, with a trapper, cross-country to the Cimarron River in Oklahoma, where he was severely ill and endangered by Indians, but eventually got back to Fort Smith in late September or early October. He returned to Philadelphia by way of New Orleans.

In 1822 Thomas Nuttall was appointed curator of Harvard University Botanic Garden in Cambridge, where he remained for twelve years. During that period, he returned to England three times, always taking seeds and plants with him, particularly those from his Arkansas collecting. But the explorer was too much in him, so he resigned his Harvard post in 1834 to accompany a friend, Captain Nathaniel Wyeth, on a transcontinental expedition to set up posts for the Columbia River Fishing and Trading Co. The route, instead of proceeding up the Missouri River, went west along the Nebraska River and the north fork of the Platte. J. K. Townsend, an ornithologist accompanying the expedition, reported that Nuttall always rode ahead, "fearful that the company would trample some prize underfoot." Always alert for Indians, they continued to follow a network of rivers and stopped to build a trading post on the Snake River, but then ran out of provisions; even the horses were dying. They eventually reached the Boise River and thence the Columbia. During this time Nuttall collected "nearly a thousand species" of plants. He endured swamped boats when going down the Columbia and had to dry out specimens, but his reward came when he found mountain dogwood (*Cornus nuttallii*). He spent the winter of 1834–35 in Hawaii aboard Captain Wyeth's brig, returned to the Columbia River in the spring of 1835, and spent six months covering much of the ground that David Douglas had covered. In 1836 he started homeward by way of California and Cape Horn. In San Diego he awaited the arrival of the brig *Alert*, on which the former Harvard student Henry Dana gained experience for what became the classic *Two Years Before the Mast*. Dana was startled, indeed, to find the familiar ex-Harvard professor on the opposite side of the continent, dressed like a boatman and collecting pebbles and shells along a beach. *Alert* arrived in Staten Island, and by September Nuttall was back in Boston.

In 1841 he inherited his uncle's house with the stipulation that he live in it nine months of each year, so Nuttall reluctantly returned to England. He went back to Philadelphia once (1847–48), cultivated his favorite American plants at his home in England, and died in 1859. A dominant theme in Thomas Nuttall's life was his great love for America, not stated as such but revealed by action, dedication, and persistence. He was physically not strong, but the forces that drove him seem monumental in comparison to most men. He wrote in his journal on March 22, 1819:

One of the wake-robins (*Erigeron glabellum, E. glabellus*). From Curtis, *The Botanical Magazine*, London (vol. 56, plate 2923), 1829.
ROBERT RUBIC

Arkansa coreopsis (*Coreopsis tinctora*). A widespread annual and common garden plant. Discovery of this coreopsis is credited to Thomas Nuttall. From Curtis, *The Botanical Magazine,* London (vol. 51, plate 2512), 1824.
ROBERT RUBIC

Who can be insensible to the beauty of the verdant hill and valley, to the sublimity of the clouded mountain, the fearful precipice, or the torrent of the cataract. Even bald and moss-grown rocks, without the aid of sculpture, forcibly inspire us with that veneration which we justly owe to the high antiquity of nature, and which appears to arise no less from a solemn and intuitive reflection on their vast capacity for duration, contrasted with that transient scene in which we ourselves only appear to act a momentary part.

John Bradbury

John Bradbury (1764/5–1823) was born in Stalybridge, England; the date is not clearly recorded. At an early age he became interested in the natural world, particularly that of plants. Although he had to leave school to work in the cotton mills, he studied Linnaeus and at the age of eighteen established an evening school, setting himself up as teacher. By the time he was twenty-two his writings had attracted the attention of the leading English scientist Sir Joseph Banks. Bradbury traveled to London, where he was received with enthusiasm and made a member of the Linnaean Society. In 1809 Bradbury came to America with a letter of introduction to Thomas Jefferson, arriving at Monticello on August 6. Although his cotton-merchant sponsors intended that Bradbury make New Orleans the center of his searches for cotton-producing land, Thomas Jefferson persuaded him otherwise and wrote a letter of introduction for Bradbury to William Clark, superintendent of Indian affairs for the Louisiana (later Missouri) Territory, who was based in Saint Louis.

Monticello, Aug. 16, 09.

Dear Sir:

This will be handed to you [mss. torn] Mr. Bradbury, an English botanist, who proposes to take St. Louis in his botanizing tour. He came recommended to me by mr. Roscoe of Liverpool, so well known by his histories of Lorenzo of Medicie & Leo X who is president of the Botanical Society of Liverpool. mr. Bradbury comes out of their employ, & having kept him here about ten days, I have had an opportunity of knowing that besides being a botanist of the first order, he is a man of entire worth and correct conduct. as such, I recommend him to your notice, advice & patronage, while within your government or its confines. perhaps you can consult no abler hand on your Western botanical observations. . . . (Reprinted in "A Sketch of the Life of John Bradbury, including His Unpublished Correspondence with Thomas Jefferson," by Rodney H. True, *Proceedings of the American Philosophical Society,* vol. LXVIII, no. 2 [Philadelphia, 1929], from the Jefferson Papers, Library of Congress, Series V, vol. 16, no. 7[k].)

Rodney True comments as follows: "This change in plan, seen in the light of subsequent events was probably a very significant decision for Bradbury. Had he gone to New Orleans, as the cotton-consuming patrons desired, he would have been virtually their agent at that source of supply. In deciding to follow the call of the wild, he became the explorer and botanist, at times unsupported and in distress, never long at rest."

Bradbury set out for Saint Louis, first going to Philadelphia, where he met Thomas Nuttall, in whom Professor Benjamin S. Barton had taken so much interest. According to True, "Barton had practically made Nuttall over during the short period of acquaintance, changing the journeyman printer into a promising young botanist, so at the time of Bradbury's arrival, Nuttall was ready for greater undertakings. He joined Bradbury and together they proceeded to St. Louis where they arrived on December 31, 1809." During the following spring and summer, Bradbury made several excursions of a hundred miles or so radius from Saint Louis, from which he collected enough plants so that he had a significant shipment to send to the Liverpool Botanic Garden. In March 1811, with Nuttall, Bradbury started up the Missouri River with a group organized by the Pacific Fur Company (this is the expedition made famous by Washington Irving in his *Astoria,* published in 1836). They traveled about 1,800 miles from Saint Louis to the Grand River (Fort Pierre?), and from there, with Ramsey Crooks, Bradbury went on another 200 miles to the fur-trading post at Mandan (near Bismarck, North Dakota). He noted in *Travels in the Interior of America in the years 1809, 1810, and 1811. . . . ,* 1817:

March 28th.— . . . we stopped in the forenoon, about a league above the mouth of Papillon Creek, and I availed myself of this opportunity to visit the bluffs four or five miles distant from us, on the northeast side. On approaching them, I found an extensive lake running along their base, across which I waded, the water in no part reaching higher than my breast. This lake had evidently been in former times the course of the river: its surface was much covered with aquatic plants, amongst which were *Nelumbium luteum* and *Hydropeltis purpurea;* on the broad leaves of the former, a great number of water snakes were basking, which on my approach darted into the water. On gaining the summit of the bluffs, I was amply repaid by the grandeur of the scene that suddenly opened to my view, and by the acquisition of a number of new plants. On looking into the valley of the Missouri from an elevation of about 250 feet, the view was magnificent; the bluffs can be seen for more than thirty miles, stretching to the north-eastward in a right line, their summits varied by an infinity of undulations. The flat valley of the river, about six or seven miles in breadth, is partly prairie, but interspersed with clumps of the finest trees, through the intervals of which could be seen the majestic but muddy Missouri. The scene towards the interior of the country was extremely singular: it presents to the view a countless number of little green hills, apparently sixty or eighty feet in perpendicular height, and so steep, that it was with much difficulty I could ascend them; some were so acutely pointed, that two people would have found it difficult to stand on the top at the same time. I wandered among these mountains in miniature until late in the afternoon, when I recrossed the lake, and arrived at the boats soon after sunset.

April 30th.—I set out with Mr. Crooks at sunrise, for the wintering house, and travelled nearly a mile on a low piece of ground, covered with long grass: at its termination we ascended a small elevation, and entered on a plain of about eight miles in length, and from two and a half to three miles in breadth. As the old grass had been burned in the autumn, it was now covered with the most beautiful verdure, intermixed with flowers. It was also adorned with clumps of trees, sufficient for ornament, but too few to intercept the sight: in the intervals we counted nine flocks of elk and deer feeding. . . .

Rather than traveling with the Astorian group to the Pacific, Bradbury returned to Saint Louis, arriving on July 9. There he found a letter from Liverpool informing him that the supporting group would make no more payments to him. Since he had a great mass not only of herbarium material but living specimens from his journey, he obtained a piece of land near Saint Louis where he planted the living material. Almost immediately on completing the job, he came down with a fever that did not abate until late November. Fortunately, he received the good news that the Liverpool Botanic Garden was forwarding the payment withheld and informing him that the Garden had obtained over a thousand potted specimens and great number of seedlings from the shipment Bradbury had sent in 1810.

On December 5, Bradbury set out for New Orleans, where he arrived on January 13, 1812. (The account, in his *Travels,* of the earthquake he experienced on the Mississippi on December 15–16 is hair-raising.) Unable to get passage to England because of the outbreak of the War of 1812, he sailed for New York. In a letter to Thomas Jefferson from Wardsbridge (now Montgomery, near Newburgh) in January 1816 he adds the postscript, "My discoveries in Botany have been published in England and are considered valuable."

The tragedy in this saga is that the Liverpool Botanic Garden, not too wisely, lent Bradbury's specimens to Frederick Pursh, who published *Florae Americae Septentrionalis,* 1814. As True records:

Here appear described from Bradbury's material 39 new species credited to Bradbury only by

Mexican-hat or prairie coneflower *(Ratibida columnifera,* published here as *Rudbeckia columnaris)* is credited to Thomas Nuttall in Curtis's *Botanical Magazine,* but John Bradbury is also known to have sent early specimens to the Liverpool Botanic Garden in 1810. Unfortunately many of his discoveries were published by the less-than-scrupulous Frederick Pursh in *Florae Americae Septentrionalis,* 1814, and Bradbury was not duly credited. From Curtis, *The Botanical Magazine,* London (vol. 38, plate 1601), 1813.
ROBERT RUBIC

including the name of the collector with the descriptions. Bradbury felt himself ignored and practically defrauded by Pursh, an opinion shared by his fellow collector, Nuttall. Roscoe's part (Liverpool Botanic Garden) in turning the material over to Pursh seems curiously enough not to have called forth the outspoken resentment directed against Pursh. Both of them in other places questioned Pursh's botanical morals which came eventually to be seriously challenged by Baldwin, Short and others.

To salvage what he could, Bradbury evidently returned to England to publish his *Travels.* The 1817 edition was so popular that a second edition was published in 1819. Practically all of Bradbury's resources had been expended in preparing his book for publication, so when an American sea captain of past acquaintance found him in such a state, he provided free passage to America for Bradbury and his family in 1817 or early in 1818. They returned to the Saint Louis area. Throughout his accounts of travel in this country, Bradbury (like Nuttall) reveals great love for it and finds the openness of Americans, both immigrant and native, refreshing, generous, and friendly as compared to the nineteenth-century class-consciousness of England. At heart, both Bradbury and Nuttall became Americans, as in many ways did David Douglas.

While few details of Bradbury's later life and of his death are known, some evidence is given by Edwin James (*Account of an Expedition from Pittsburgh to the Rocky Mountains, 1819–20,* 1823):

The grassy plains to the west of St. Louis are ornamented with many beautiful flowering herbaceous plants. . . . It is here that Mr. John Bradbury, so long and so advantagely known as a botanist, and by his travels into the interior of America, is preparing to erect his habitation. . . . This amiable gentleman lost no opportunity during our stay . . . to make our residence there agreeable to us. . . . (May 1819).

An item appearing in the *Missouri Republican,* May 7, 1823, states:

Died; at Middletown, Kentucky, on the 16th of March last, after a short illness, Mr. John Bradbury. Mr. Bradbury is known to the scientific world as among the first botanists and mineralogists. His knowledge in science generally was esteemed valuable. Never was there a better companion, nor a more sincere friend.

David Douglas, Horticulturist

David Douglas (1799–1834) was more horticulturally oriented than Thomas Nuttall and the strictly botanist collectors. Born in Perthshire, Scotland, he was apprenticed as a gardener and managed to get a good education and an appointment to the staff of the Glasgow Botanic Garden. He became a collector for the Horticultural Society and arrived in New York in the summer of 1823. In Philadelphia he met Nuttall, saw Bartram's garden, and visited nurseries; he then left for Albany and Buffalo and traveled along Lake Erie to Amherstburg, near Detroit. In September 1823 he records (*Journal of David Douglas During His Travels in America, 1823–27,* 1914):

September 16th.—. . . This is what I might term my first day in America. The trees in the woods were of astonishing magnitude. The soil, in general, over which we passed was a very rich black earth, and seemed to be formed of decomposed vegetables [vegetation, particularly herbaceous] . . . . The woods consisted of *Quercus* (several species, some of immense magnitude); *Juglans cathartica, J. nigra* (immensely large), *J. porcina;* in dry places *Fagus,* and on its roots a species of *Orobanche;* also a species under oaks very different from the former one. Four miles east of Amherstburg I observed a species of rose of strong growth, the wood resembling *multiflora,* having strong thorns. All the tender shoots and leaves were eaten off by cattle or sheep, which prevented me from knowing it. I gathered seeds of some species of *Liatris,* which, along with *Helianthus, Solidago, Aster, Eupatorium,* and *Vernonia* form the majority of which I had an opportunity of seeing in perfection. In a field east of Amherstburg grew spontaneously *Gentiana Saponaria* (?) and *crinita,* and I secured seeds. Towards mid-afternoon the rain fell in torrents, urging us to leave the woods drenched in wet.

September 19th.—. . . In a small marsh grew *Chelone glabra,* var. *alba,* a fine plant; it had not seeds, I therefore took plants. In the same place *Coreopsis* sp. 1 Herb., flowers a fine bright yellow, growing in water; a Manong, a species of *Bidens,* which had no seeds. On my way home, two miles from Sandwich, among underwood grew a *Phlox* 18 inches high, leaves linear, opposite, and having flower large in proportion to the plant; soil, sandy peat or nearly all sand. I was much pleased with this, it had no seeds; I of course took plants. On the same place *Gerardia* sp. looked like *quercifolia,* plenty of seeds but no flower. I wish they may grow. *Neottia* or *Satyrium* in peat. *Cypripedium* in sandy peat soil among bushes.

September 23rd.—I made an excursion across the river to the Michigan Territory, at which place I found several species of *Liatris,* a *Smilax* of a curious appearance, a species of *Elymus* very strong in the marshes, *Lobelia inflata* and *syphilitica* in wet places; in a dry part of the wood among dead leaves *Botrychium, Arum triphyllum, Pothos foetidus.* These plants struck me as singular; they, without fail, in most cases, frequent moist places. I have not seen *Sarracenia* in the Upper Province. *Trillium* is also scarce.

September 24th.—. . . Several *Liatris* on fine marl, tall, colour bright red, almost scarlet; a specimen of *Lilium canadense* in sandy peat soil. I here gathered a promiscuous group of several things but my time is so short that I cannot insert them.

September 25th.—I packed my gleanings of plants and seeds and specimens, and stood in readiness for the steamboat from Detroit, which came in the afternoon.

September 30th.—This morning before daylight I was up and at the Falls [Niagara]. I am, like most who have seen them, sensitively impressed with their grandeur. Out of the cliffs of the rock grow Red Cedar, *Juglans amara,* and *Quercus.* On the channel of the river I picked up an *Astragalus* and beside it a Viola, both in seed; the *Viola* grew in sand and its seed-pods were buried among it. I crossed below the Falls to the American side, and then to the island called Goat Island. It is partly covered with woods of large dimensions; the soil is variable, part rich and part sand and gravel. The sugar maple, *Acer saccharinum,* on the brink of the rocks grew very large; they had all been tapped or bled and still seemed uncommonly vigorous. There were a few pines of two species, but had no cones. *Botrychium,*

Lupine *(Lupinus nanus)* and mariposa tulip, also lily- or globe-tulip (now *Calochortus albus)* are included in this bouquet introduced by David Douglas. From George Bentham, "Report . . . Hardy Ornamental Plants raised in the Horticultural Society's garden from seeds received from Mr. David Douglas . . . 1831, 32, 33." *Horticultural Transactions,* London (vol. 1, series 2), 1834.
ROBERT RUBIC

Leptosiphon (now *Linanthus*) and bird's eyes or blue-eyed Gilia *(Gilia tricolor)*, introduced by David Douglas. From George Bentham, "Report . . . Hardy Ornamental Plants." ROBERT RUBIC

two species in shady parts of the wood in decayed leaves; two species of *Orobanche,* in dry places also among leaves. *Trillium* seemed to be plentiful, but the leaves being decayed, I could not get as many as I would like. *Arum triphyllum, Dracontium* sp., and *Pothos foetidus*: I was not a little surprised to see *Pothos* in a dry place; they had perfected seeds. *Rhus Vernix* in conjunction with some species of *Smilax,* and other species of *Rhus* clad the trunks of the large trees.

After returning to New York, in December 1823, Douglas went back to England. He was not to be there for long, however, for the Horticultural Society had plans for him. He left London July 25, 1824, boarded a Hudson's Bay Company ship, and set out for the Pacific Northwest. Douglas's *Journal,* in 1825, continues:

April 7th.—. . . At four we came to anchor in Baker's Bay, on the north side of the river.

Several shots of the cannon were immediately fired to announce our arrival to the establishment 7 miles up the river, but were not answered. Thus my long and tedious voyage of 8 months 14 days from England terminated. The joy of viewing land, the hope of in a few days ranging through the long wished-for spot and the pleasure of again resuming my wonted employment may be readily calculated. We spent the evening with great mirth and at an early hour went to sleep. . . . With truth I may count this one of the happy moments of my life. As might naturally be supposed to enjoy the sight of land, free from the excessive motion and noise of the ship—from all deprived nearly nine months—was to me truly a luxury. The ground on the south side of the river is low, covered thickly with wood, chiefly *Pinus canadensis, P. balsamea,* and a species which may prove to be *P. taxifolia.* The north (Cape Disappointment) is a remarkable promontory, elevation about 700 feet above the sea, covered with wood of the same kinds as on the other side.

April 8th.—Constant heavy rain, cold, thermometer 47°. Saturday the 9th in company with Mr. Scouler I went on shore on Cape Disappointment as the ship could not proceed up the river in consequence of heavy rains and thick fogs. On stepping on the shore *Gaultheria Shallon* was the first plant I took in my hands. So pleased was I that I could scarcely see anything but it. . . . It grows most luxuriantly on the margins of woods, particularly near the ocean. . . . *Rubus spectabilis* was also abundant; both these delightful plants in blossom. In the woods were several species of *Vaccinium,* but not yet in blossom, a species of *Tiarella* and *Heuchera* in flower.

April 19th.—. . . I left the mouth of the river; at 8 o'clock morning in a small boat with one Canadian and six Indians; we made only forty miles, having no wind and a very strong current against us. We slept in the canoe, which we pulled up on the beach. . . . We started at three o'clock the following morning and reached our destination at ten on Wednesday night. The scenery in many parts is exceedingly grand; twenty-seven miles from the ocean the country is undulating, the most part covered with wood, chiefly pine. On both sides of the river are extensive plains of deep rich alluvial soil, with a thick herbage of herbaceous plants. Here the country becomes mountainous, and on the banks of the river the rocks rise perpendicularly to the height of several hundred feet in some parts, over which are some fine waterfalls. . . . The country continues mountainous as far as the lower branch of the Multnomah [Willamette] river. . . .

August 16th.—. . . My residence is on the north bank of the river twelve miles below Point Vancouver (90 from the ocean), the spot where the officer of his squadron discontinued their survey of the river. The place is called Fort Vancouver. . . . On my arrival a tent was kindly offered, having no houses yet built, which I occupied for some weeks; a lodge of deerskin was then made for me which soon became too small by the augmenting of my collection and being ill adapted for drying my plants and seeds. I am now . . . in a hut made of bark of *Thuya occidentalis* which most likely will be my winter lodging. I have been only three nights in a house since my arrival, the three first on shore. On my journeys I have a tent where it can be carried, which rarely can be done; sometimes I sleep in one, sometimes under a canoe turned upside down, but most commonly under the shade of a pine tree without anything.

[A list of plants is added to each day's notes. The list for this entry:]

Iris sp., perennial; flowers blue; a small plant, 6 inches to a foot high; in fertile plains, near the margin of rivulets; abundant. S.

Allied to *Lithospermum*; annual; flowers rose coloured; dry gravelly soil; plentiful.

—(?); suffructicose; abundant in dry places.

[*bis*] Allied to *Lithospermum*; perennial; flowers dingy-white; a foot to 18 inches high; plains in rich soils; abundant; a fine plant. S.

Ornithogalum (?); flowers yellow; bulbs used by the natives as an emetic; perennial; near Point Vancouver, in open gravelly soils, plentiful in rich plains; a fine plant. S.

—(?), what Pursh has given as *Lilium pudicum*; stigma three-cleft, which removes it from that genus; perennial. Bulbs of this plant are eaten in a boiled state by the natives. Abundant on the plains and near the outskirts of woods. Bulbs of this are sent home in a jar among dry sand.

Throughout the time that David Douglas was in the Pacific Northwest, he referred many times to *Gaultheria shallon* (see *Journal* entry for April 8, above), which came to be his favorite plant or, at the very least, the one that he admired most among several favorites. It is the lemonleaf so common in florists' shops today, where it has been favored for many years because of its clean, broad evergreen leaves and arching branches, which often are tinged with red.

For two years, using Fort Vancouver as his base, Douglas explored the Columbia and Multnomah rivers and made two trips to the Cascade Mountains. The ship on which he had sailed from England had returned from the north, so Douglas was able to send home a large collection of seeds and plant specimens, as well as notes and specimens of birds and mammals. He traveled about 2,000 miles that first year and almost 4,000 the second.

April 20th.—. . . arrived at Fort Vancouver, ninety miles from the sea, a few miles below Point Vancouver, the spot where the officers of that expedition terminated the survey of the river in 1792. The scenery from this place is sublime—high well-wooded hills, mountains covered with perpetual snow, extensive natural meadows and plains of deep fertile alluvial deposit covered with a rich sward of grass and a profusion of flowering plants. The most remarkable mountains are Mounts Hood, St. Helens, Vancouver, and Jefferson, which are at all seasons covered with snow as low down as the summit of the hills by which they are

One of the most spectacular of the plates in Bentham's report on Douglas introductions includes *Calochortus splendens* and *Triteleia laxa,* sometimes known as trout-lily. These plates from Bentham are a tribute to Douglas's discerning eye. From George Bentham, "Report . . . Hardy Ornamental Plants."
ROBERT RUBIC

surrounded. From this period till May 10th my labour in the neighbourhood of this place was well rewarded by *Ribes sanguineum, Berberis Aquifolium, B. glumacea,* (B. *nervosa,* Pursh), *Acer macrophyllum, Scilla esculenta, Pyrola aphylla, Caprifolium ciliosum,* and a multitude of other plants. I cannot pass over the grandeur of *Lupinus polyphyllus* covering immense tracts of low land on the banks of streams, with here and there a white variety. This beautiful plant attains the height of 6 to 8 feet where partly overflowered by water. . . . We had abundance of salmon brought to us by the native tribes, which was purchased cheap and which we found excellent. I returned to Fort Vancouver at the end of the month, having increased my collection by seventy-five species of plants, a few birds and insects, and four quadrupeds.

June 20th.—. . . [Near Walla Walla] Scarcely had half an hour gone when a dark cloud passed over me and a dreadful thunderstorm commenced, with lightning in massy sheets, mixed with forked flashes and hail and large pieces of ice, and the thunder resounding through the deep valleys below. In the dying gusts of the storm one of the most sublime spectacles in Nature presented itself: the declining sun had just partially gilt the top of the snowy mountains, and below a magnificent rainbow was nearly a perfect circle. All tended to impress the mind with reverential awe. . . .

I contented myself by botanising over the eastern declivities of the mountains for a few days, and returned to the Columbia on Sunday the 25th. All this time, toil, and some vexation, were not spent without being productive of some pleasure. In those untrodden regions on the verge of eternal snow were *Paeonia Brownii,* the first ever found in America; and at a lower elevation the whole declivities of the mountains were covered with *Lupinus Sabinii* (whose beautiful golden blossoms gave a tint to the country that reminded me of *Spartium scoparium*), *Trifolium megacephalum* (*Lupinaster macrocephalus,* Pursh), *Trifolium altissimum,* and several new species of *Phlox.*

During the summer of 1826, after exploring several of the tributaries of the Columbia, Douglas remained for several weeks in Walla Walla, from which he made excursions into the desert. Here he began having eye problems and complained of dimness; the light reflecting from the ground was particularly irritating. Nevertheless, he continued, crossing and crisscrossing the route that Lewis and Clark had traveled twenty years before, and reported that he had collected ninety-seven distinct species of plants and forty-five "papers" (packets made by folding paper) of seed. Hearing that a ship was leaving for England on September 1, he returned to Fort Vancouver in time to see his shipment stowed aboard and homeward bound.

Within three weeks Douglas was off again, this time following the Willamette Valley. He was in search of a particular pine he had heard about from the Indians and was eager to collect. It was a grueling trip, Douglas carrying his collections on his back. But, with the help of an Indian guide, he found the tree he had sought: sugar or giant pine (*Pinus lambertiana*).

September 24th.—. . . I had left my new guide at the camp and proceeded in a south-east direction, and had only crossed a low hill when I came to abundance of *Pinus Lambertiana.* I put myself in possession of a great number of perfect cones, but circumstances obliged me to leave the ground hastily with only three—a party of eight Indians endeavoured to destroy me. I returned to the camp, got the horses saddled and made a speedy retreat.

December 20th.—. . . at the Fort [Vancouver], I found letters for me from London, which were pleasant. I remained here till December 9th, when I undertook a voyage to the coast in hope of replacing some articles lost last winter. This was a still more unfortunate undertaking, for I had my canoe wrecked; and from the wet and cold returned home sick, having added nothing to my collection save one new species of *Ledum.* This winter was spent in the same way as the former.

March 20th.—By the annual express . . . I left Fort Vancouver for England, where I spent, if not many comfortable days, many pleasant ones. Though happy of the opportunity of returning to my native land, yet I confess I certainly left with regret a country so exceedingly interesting.

I walked the whole distance from this place to Fort Colville on the Kettle Falls, which occupied twenty-five days. Not a day passed but brought something new or interesting either in botany or zoology. The beautiful *Erythronium maximum* and *Claytonia lanceolata* were in full bloom among the snow.

The "annual express" referred to by Douglas was by no means an express in today's terms. Rather, it was the Hudson's Bay Company's regular spring link to York Factory on Hudson Bay, where ships for England arrived during the ice-free season, particularly to pick up furs for the European market. It took the group two months to reach Jasper House via the Columbia River and overland through the Athabasca Pass. Even during this season, Douglas was always alert and collected many seeds of conifers as well as other plants along the way. Entries in his *Journal* include:

April 28th.—Having the whole of my journals, a tin box of seeds, and a shirt or two tied up in a bundle, we commenced our march across the mountains in an easterly course, first entering a low swampy piece of ground about 3 miles long, knee deep of water and covered with rotten ice through which we sunk to the knees at every step. Crossed a deep muddy creek and entered a point of wood principally consisting of pine—*P[inus] balsamea, P. nigra, P. alba,* and *P. Strobus,* and *Thuya plicata.* About eleven we entered the snow, which was 4 to 7 feet deep, moist and soft, and together with the fallen timber, made heavy walking on snow-shoes. Camped on the west side of the middle branch of the Columbia. Of animals we saw only two species of squirrels.

May 1st.—. . . At the elevation of 4800 feet vegetation no longer exists—not so much as a lichen of any kind to be seen, 1200 feet of eternal ice. The view from the summit is of that cast too awful to afford pleasure—nothing as far as the eye can reach in every direction but mountains towering above each other, rugged beyond all description; the dazzling reflection from the snow, the heavenly arena of the solid glacier, and the rainbow-like tints of its shattered fragments, together with the enormous icicles suspended from the perpendicular rocks; the majestic but terrible avalanche hurtling down from the southerly exposed rocks producing a crash, and groans through the distant valleys, only equalled by an earthquake. Such gives us a sense of the stupendous and wondrous works of the Almighty.

After leaving Jasper House, the party continued on to Edmonton, where Douglas remained for ten days, leaving on May 31. The route eastward was via the Saskatchewan River to Lake Winnipeg.

May 21st to 31st.—Around Edmonton the country is woodless and uninteresting. Embarked in Mr. Stuart's boat, in company with others, to Fort Carlton House. Our mode of travelling gave me little time to botanise; the only times were the short stay made to breakfast, the dusk of the evening before camping, and the most when a delay was made for the purpose of hunting buffalo and red deer. . . .

Among a variety of the plants not before in my herbarium were *Astragalus pectinatus, A. Drummondii, Phlox Hoodii, Thermopsis rhombifolia, Hedysarum Mackenzii, Astragalus succulentus, A. caryocarpus,* and seven species of *Salix.* . . .

At Carlton House (now Carlton, Saskatchewan), in June, Douglas met Thomas Drummond:

. . . At Carlton House I had the pleasure to meet Mr. Drummond . . . who spent the greater part of his time in the Rocky Mountains contiguous to the sources of the Rivers Athabasca and Columbia.

Mr. Drummond had a princely collection. I had intended to cross the plain from this place to Swan and Red Rivers, but from the hostile disposition of the Stone Indians deemed it unsafe. I descended to Cumberland House. . . .

We proceeded under sail to Norway House with an open sheet of water. The shores of the lake are clothed with diminutive trees, *Pinus alba, nigra, microcarpa, Betula papyracea, nigra, Populus trepida,* with sphagnous swamps of *Ledum, Kalmia,* and *Andromeda,* and near springs or pools strong herbage of *Carex.* On the 16th we arrived at Norway House, where I had letters from England. The following day George Simpson, Esq., the resident Governor of the Hudson's Bay Company, arrived, from whom I had great kindness. A few days were spent here, when Captain Sir John Franklin arrived, who politely offered me a passage in his canoe through the lake as far as the mouth of Winnipeg River on my way to Red River, which was gladly embraced. . . . The following day [June 10] I proceeded to the settlement on the Red River, where I arrived on the 12th. I took up my abode with Donald McKenzie, Esq., Governor of the Colony. . . . During a month's residence I formed a small herbarium of 288 species, many of which were new to me, and I felt truly happy at having devoted a little time to it; for several plants were added to the flora, and had I stayed with Mr. Drummond or Dr. Richardson on the Saskatchewan these would have been omitted. I left with Mr. Hamlyn, the surgeon to the colony, had a somewhat tedious passage through the lake, and had the pleasure to arrive at York Factory, Hudson's Bay, where I was kindly received by John George McTavish, Esq., Chief Factor, who had had the kindness to get made for me some clothing, my travelling stock being completely worn out.

Here my labours ended; and I may be allowed to state, when the natural difficulties of passing through a new country are taken into view, the disposition of the native tribes—in fact, the varied insufferable inconveniences that daily present themselves—I have great reason to look on myself as highly favoured. All that my feeble exertions may have done only stimulated us to future exertion. The whole of my botanical collection, save a few that came intimately within the Society's Minute, were, agreeably

Clarkia, a genus with several species, was discovered in California by David Douglas and named in honor of William Clark of Northwest Passage fame. Many double forms in many colors are popular greenhouse and garden plants. From Sydenham Edwards, *The Botanical Register,* London (vol. 14, plate 1575), 1833.
ROBERT RUBIC

with my anxious wishes, given for publication in the forthcoming American Flora from the pen of Dr. Hooker.

I sailed from Hudson's Bay on September 15th and arrived at Portsmouth [England] on October 11th [1827], having enjoyed a most gratifying trip.

Douglas was well received; he had collected so much seed, it was reported, that the Horticultural Society had difficulty distributing all of it. Many now-familiar garden plants, previously known only to botanists, were made available to everyone: California poppy (*Eschscholzia californica*), elegant Clarkia (*Clarkia elegans,* now *C. unguiculata*), musk flower (*Mimulus moschatus*), blue-pod lupine (*Lupinus polyphyllus*). Douglas also introduced into cultivation the excellent broad-leaf evergreen Oregon holly-grape (*Mahonia aquifolium*). But probably most admired at the time was flowering currant (*Ribes sanguineum*). His name will forever be most recognized, however, for Douglas fir (*Pseudotsuga taxifolia*), which is not a true fir (*Abies* spp.). Beginning students, knowledgeable of Latin, had no trouble with this name because for them it translated "false Hemlock (*Tsuga*) with Yew (*Taxus*)-like foliage." Alas, taxonomists—not often beloved by horticulturists—have decided that, by right of nomenclatural priority, it is correctly *Pseudotsuga menziesii.* And so it is.

In October 1830, Douglas again sailed for America with a commission from the Horticultural Society and surveying instruments from the Colonial Office. His assignment to map the Columbia Valley resulted in a definitive work that is highly regarded today.

His love for Hawaii and California drew him there for winter respites, but he collected plants wherever he went. At that time California belonged to Mexico, but after obtaining permits Douglas began collecting there in 1831. As at the Canadian trading posts, he was welcomed at the missions and he found the missionaries cooperative and generously helpful. He returned to Monterey hoping for a ship bound for the Columbia, but since none came he remained in the area through spring and summer, 1832, alert for possible passage. Finally, in August, he went to Hawaii and from there sent home his California collections, which included many now-common garden plants: creamcup (*Platystemon californicus*), baby blue-eyes (*Nemophila menziesii*), scarlet delphinium (*Delphinium cardinale*), godetia (*Godetia quadrivulenta,* now a subspecies of *Clarkia purpurea*), and others.

In October Douglas returned to the Columbia River, where he continued surveying. He complained of continuing eye problems from the glare of snow and the desert floor, which he constantly scanned for new plants. His ability to discover new plants in the complex foliages of familiar plants was considered awesome; perhaps he was afraid that he would miss a plant if he wore glasses. He attempted another trip inland. After losing his botanical collections, journals, and personal belongings when his canoe was smashed, he stayed in Walla Walla, from where he made new excursions. He attempted to climb Mount Hood and finally returned to Fort Vancouver in September. From there he returned to the Sandwich Islands (now Hawaii); after spending Christmas in Honolulu, he arrived on the

The California poppy *(Eschscholzia californica)* is a popular garden plant wherever it can be grown throughout the world. It and its near-species *(E. mexicana)* are common in the west and southwest, sometimes carpeting the hills and deserts with brilliant color. From Curtis, *The Botanical Magazine,* London (vol. 56, plate 2887), 1829.
ROBERT RUBIC

big island, Hawaii, on December 31. He climbed Mauna Loa and Mauna Kea, continuing to collect plants at every opportunity.

January 23 [1834]—The morning was deliciously cool and clear, with a light breeze. Immediately on passing through a narrow belt of wood, where the timber was large, and its trunks matted with parasitic Ferns, I arrived at a tract of ground, over which there was but a scanty covering of soil above the lava, interspersed with low bushes and Ferns. Here I beheld one of the grandest scenes imaginable;—Mouna Roa [Mauna Loa] reared his bold front, covered with snow, far above the region of verdure, while Mouna Kuāh [Mauna Kea] was similarly clothed, to the timber region on the South side, while the summit was cleared of the snow that had fallen on the nights of the 12th and two following days. The district of Hido [Hilo], "Byron's Bay," which I had quitted the previous day, presented, from its great moisture, a truly lovely appearance, contrasting in a striking manner with the country where I then stood, and which extended to the sea, whose surface bore evident signs of having been repeatedly ravaged by volcanic fires. In the distance, to the South-West, the dense black cloud which overhangs the great volcano, attests, amid the otherwise unsullied purity of the sky, the mighty operations at present going on in that immense laboratory. (*Journal, Appendix II*)

The last entry in David Douglas's *Journal* is dated January 30. Sometime after that he returned to Honolulu and then went back to the island of Hawaii, arriving at its northernmost extreme. He had heard of a trail from Kohala to Hilo, which he wished to travel, collecting plants along the way, of course. As with Captain Cook before him, it was on this island that he met his death. The prevalent version of the story is that he fell into a pit trap and was trampled and gored to death by one of the wild cattle.

In a well-documented, unpublished manuscript, "The Mystery of Kaluakauka," 1985, Jean Greenwell of the Kona Historical Society reports that Douglas spent the night before his death, July 14, 1834, at the lodge of a bullock hunter "by the name of Edward Gurney, called Ned. . . . Gurney made his living by trapping wild cattle that were descendants of those given King Kamehameha I by Captain Vancouver in the 1790s. . . . By the 1830s they were almost a menace on the mountain." Gurney was described, at the time, as an Englishman who had arrived in Honolulu in 1822, where he deserted ship; it also was known that he had been a convict in Australia. "By the time Douglas meets up with him," continues Mrs. Greenwell, "he was well established on Mauna Kea hunting wild animals, curing their hides and salting beef." Douglas, according to Gurney's story, left on the morning of July 14, after being warned about the traps. Later in the morning two Hawaiians who worked for Gurney reported that the *Kauka* (doctor) had fallen into one of the traps. (Douglas's little dog and belongings were nearby.) Gurney wrapped the body in hide and sent it to Hilo, where a Mr. Hall, a former bullock hunter but now a carpenter, was engaged to make a coffin. Upon viewing the body, "it struck him that the wounds did not appear to be those made by an animal. Most of the wounds were on [Douglas's] head and not over his whole body . . . where they would be if he had been trampled." Hall suggested that the doctor was murdered for his money because he was known to carry "a good amount with him." The missionaries, who had been friends of Douglas, shipped the body, in brine, to Honolulu for autopsy, where it arrived in early August "in a most offensive state." The body was examined (hastily, we may be tempted to presume) and the doctors declared that Douglas's wounds were caused by a bull and that they saw no need for further examination.

Douglas was buried at Kawaiahao Church in Honolulu; the exact location of his grave is unknown, but more than six thousand feet above the Pacific, near the site of the bullock pit on Mauna Kea, is a stone monument to this man. It stands in a grove of Douglas firs planted on the hundredth anniversary of his death. Beside the rough road, a Hawaii State Landmark marker with a likeness of King Kamehameha I states, simply, "Doctor's Pit."

The indefatigable energy of David Douglas in the face of ovewhelming odds—the accidents, illnesses, near starvation, and fading eyesight—sometimes suggests that this man was frantic, the possessor of a single-mindedness approaching insanity. Until Ned Gurney or the wild ox, nothing stopped him. Yet his contributions place him high in the pantheon of plantsmen. After him, all Englishmen looked to western America as a lode not of gold but of horticultural jewels to be treasured and grown to perfection in English rock gardens and alpine houses. If the English climate is not ideal for people, it was made so for plants. Plants from all over the world, especially those of the Pacific Northwest, grow there as if they are completely at home. Flora smiled on England and Englishmen.

Thomas Drummond: The Pacific Northwest and Texas

Thomas Drummond (c. 1790–1835), who died in Cuba the year following the death of David Douglas in Hawaii, was appointed curator at the Belfast Botanic Garden upon his return from Canada with Douglas in 1827. He served in the position for only three years, leaving to become an independent plant collector. Sponsored by the Edinburgh and Glasgow botanic gardens, he headed for Texas. Arriving in New York in April 1831, he met the American botanist John Torrey (1796–1873) and collected spring plants in the Philadelphia area, which he sent to Joseph Hooker at Kew. Eventually reaching Frederickstown, Virginia, he set out on foot across the Alleghenies to Wheeling, an easy trip for him after the Rocky Mountain experiences of his first trip. Here modern progress became a disadvantage: steamboats had replaced the small boats that were much more useful for exploring riverbanks and woodlands along the way. In Saint Louis Drummond fell ill and missed the opportunity to join a fur-trading party heading for Santa Fe and the New Mexico mountains. Nevertheless, he sent living plants to Hooker, then went to New Orleans, which became his base of operations for the next year.

From New Orleans he traveled up the Red River to Natchitoches (south of what is now Shrevesport), explored the north side of Lake Pontchartrain and Covington, then took a boat to Velasco at the mouth of the Brazos River, south of Galveston. He explored the river, upstream, to Brazoria. Surviving an epidemic of cholera, Drummond returned to

Many species of penstemon (also, old style: pentstemon) are native throughout America; the discovery of slender penstemon *(P. gracilis)* is credited to Thomas Drummond. The most spectacular species are native to the west coast and southwest and are popular in gardens throughout the world wherever they can be grown. From Curtis, *The Botanical Magazine,* London (vol. 56, plate 2945), 1829. ROBERT RUBIC

Thomas Drummond sent seeds of this phlox *(Phlox drummondii)* to England early in 1835 and is generally credited with its discovery. However, this popular phlox was first collected by Jean Louis Berlandier, who also collected a great variety of wildlife specimens in northern Mexico and Texas. ("Journeys into Mexico during the Years 1826–34." Joseph Ewan in *SIDA,* vol. 9 [4]: 381. Dallas: Southern Methodist University, 1982). From Curtis, *The Botanical Magazine,* London (vol. 62, plate 3441), 1835. ROBERT RUBIC

Velasco and went up the Brazos River again, where he planned to join a surveying party going inland. Fortunately, he changed his mind—the party was massacred—but wherever he went he collected specimens and seed. He also collected shells and anything else that might reveal the nature of the country. While he seems to have explored very little of Texas, he found many exceptionally beautiful plants that soon became garden favorites in England: a new evening primrose (*Oenothera drummondii*), poppy mallow (*Callirhoe papaver*), and the wonderful bluebell gentian (*Eustoma grandiflorum*), which suddenly seems to have been rediscovered by the American florist industry. Misnamed *Lisianthus,* it is grown as a cut flower and is widely available in New York and other cities 150 years after Drummond found it. The all-time favorite of Drummond's introductions for gardeners is the low-growing, sprightly annual phlox (*Phlox drummondii*), which Hooker named in Drummond's honor along with several other plants. One authority states that the seeds were collected near Gonzales, east of San Antonio, the year before Drummond's death, but this phlox grows in so many parts of Texas that it could have been collected almost anywhere provided seeds were ripe and ready to harvest. Thomas Drummond was so impressed with Texas that he applied for a grant of land so he could return with his family and continue collecting.

Drummond sailed for Florida in January 1835. The next news of him is in a letter addressed to the director of Kew, dated March 11, 1835, from the consul at Havana. Enclosed were a death certificate and references to a letter that was never received.

John Jeffrey, et al.

John Jeffrey (1826–1854?) is yet another of the collectors trained at the Edinburgh Botanic Garden. He arrived in Hudson Bay in 1850 and followed the usual route westward, traveling 1,200 miles on snowshoes for a portion of the distance, to Fort Vancouver. At first he was a diligent collector, sending home more than 119 species of plants: Washington lily (*Lilium washingtonianum*), canon delphinium (*D. nudicaulis*), camas (*Camassia leichtlinii*), Sierra shooting star (*Dodecathion jeffreyi*), scarlet fritillary (*Fritillaria recurva*), mountain-pride (*Penstemon newberryi*), and a campion (*Silene hookeri*).

Jeffrey sent his last shipment from San Francisco in January 1854 and then disappeared. Rumor had it that he was robbed and killed by a Mexican outcast, died of exposure in the Colorado desert, or was caught up in the gold rush and sought his fortune with a pan.

The story of plant explorers in America does not end with John Jeffrey and we are not even sure that it began with Hariot and White. There were others: John Bartram's son, William, who accompanied his father and became recognized for his wildlife illustrations (most of them now in the British Museum); the "Pilgrim Botanist" Thomas More; John Fraser, who first came to Newfoundland in 1780, later made two or three trips to Charleston, and in 1795 established a nursery in London near Sloan Square (he is credited in *Index Kewensis* with the introduction of forty-four new plants); Fraser's son, John II, who accompanied his father and later operated nurseries (after Sloan Square at Ramsgate) featuring American plants; John Lyon, who collected plants to sell for profit in London but is credited for introducing red or copper iris (*Iris fulva*), wild bleeding-heart (*Dicentra eximia*), and turtlehead (*Chelone lyonii*). And there were Fremont and Hartweg and Lobb; all contributed to the great fund of knowledge about American plants, made of them some of the most important of garden ornamentals, and provided insights into the history of America and the attitudes and dreams of the people who came here.

By today's standards, concerned as we are with rare and endangered species, we are shocked by stories of plant-collecting on such a vast scale. But the natural system is a powerful force. Shiploads of exported sassafras bark did not cause sassafras to become extinct. The collecting of *Franklinia* on the shores of the Alatamaha River may well have saved this plant from extinction; although it has not been found in the wild since, through horticultural practices it has been propagated and distributed to nearly every part of the world.

But this is not to say that we can continue to collect plants from the wild. A tradition appropriate in one era is not necessarily appropriate in another, and the threats to the natural system are massive.

There are many species of silene, campion, or catchfly throughout the U.S. Some are very showy, some hardly more than nuisance weeds. This species from Oregon and California *(S. hookeri)* discovered by Thomas Nuttall was so unusual that many other collector-botanists sent seeds to England, too. From Curtis, *The Botanical Magazine*, London (vol. 99, plate 6051), 1873.
ROBERT RUBIC

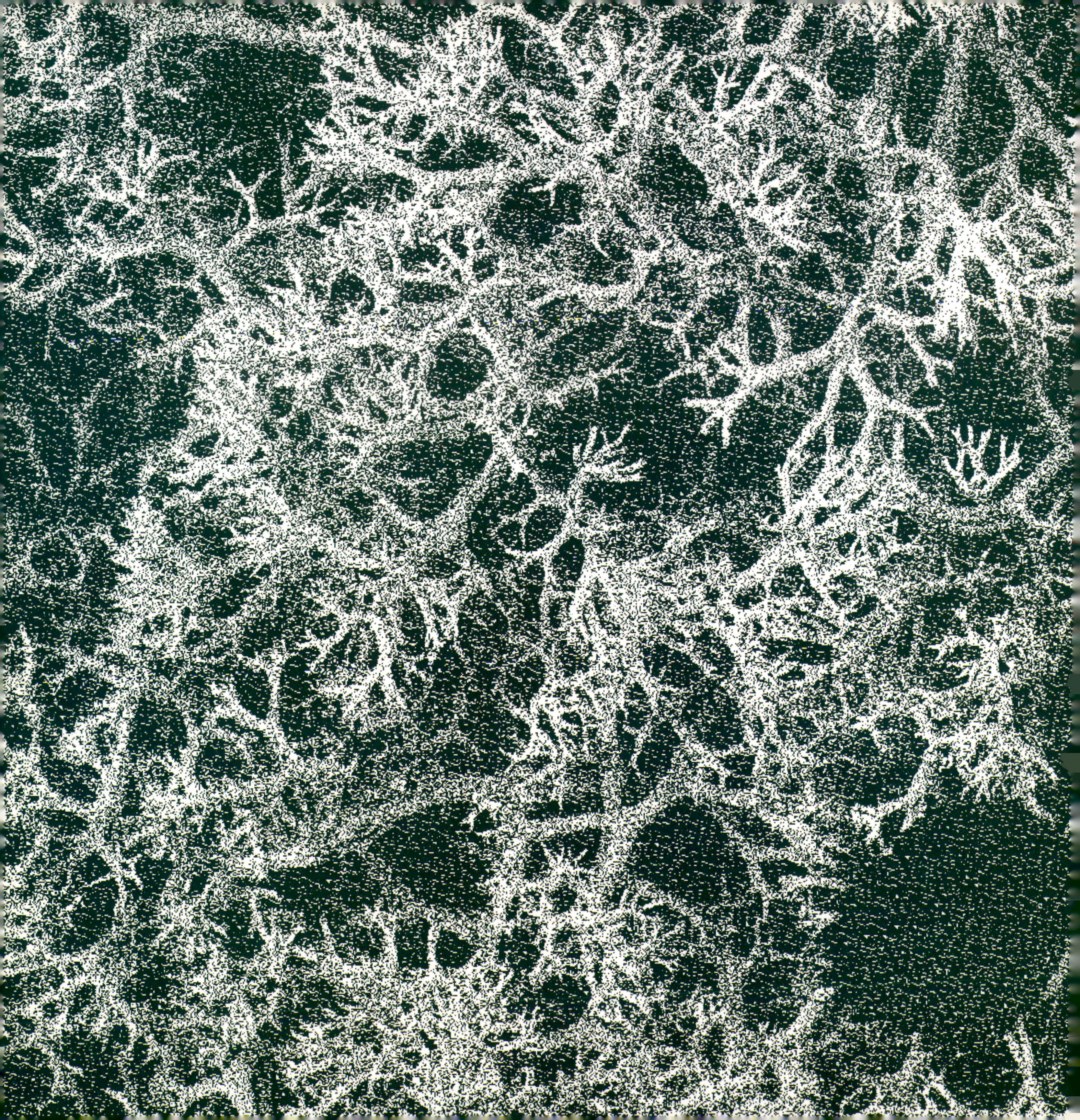

To Each a Season: North, East, South, West

Favorite Wildflowers of the Southwest

Mexican hat *(Ratibida columnifera)*, Texas. LARRY WEST

Texas bluebonnets *(Lupinus texensis)*, National Wildflower Research Center, Austin, Texas. JOSE AZEL, Contact Press Images

Often I am asked what my favorite wildflowers are. Since there are nearly five thousand species in Texas, with a great many of them found here in the Hill Country of central Texas, that is a hard question to answer. Bluebonnet would certainly be on the list, although I am a little frustrated when people know only about bluebonnets and nothing at all about the vast panoply of others.

The bluebonnet that grows here in central Texas is Lupinus texensis, *which is lush and full and blue, topped with white, and there is a little red in the upper petal. Every now and then, you will come across a white sport, which always stands out and always makes you wonder.*

Bluebonnets begin as early as March. I know that precisely because Lyndon was in the hospital in March after we returned from Washington in 1969. On the second of March, Texas Independence Day, a visitor brought us the first bluebonnet, with a big smile. It came from Llano County, where everything comes early out of the red granite soil—and, unhappily, also goes early if it is a very hot spring. In April, the bluebonnet is the Queen of the Season, reaching its zenith in about the third week, usually, and lasting into May.

Bluebonnets were sometimes also called buffalo clover. They are supposed to have sprung up in vast masses where the buffaloes roamed over the land in great herds, their feet churning the ground into dust—a good way to get soil-seed contact, which is what you must have when you are planting them! To me, bluebonnets are capricious and *elusive. We have not had great luck in propagating them at the Center; nor do many people I know have much luck. Bluebonnets belong to nature, belong to the Lord. He puts them where He wants them. Growing them is not the easiest thing, although the seeds are plentiful and have been harvested commercially for a long time. The bluebonnet is one of the very few Texas flowers that is harvested commercially, its seeds ranging in price from $3 to $24 a pound in my experience. It takes about ten to twelve pounds an acre to plant a large area, if you ask the Texas Highway Department. We at the Center think you should plant a great deal more if you want to get a good show the first year—as much as fifteen to twenty pounds an acre.*

Bluebonnets have very hard seeds, and it is said that you should scrape them or puncture them to increase the chances of germination. I wonder about that, because I think maybe that's nature's own insurance policy—a way of "hedging your bet." If there is a terribly hard, cold, dry winter or a very hot, dry, early spring, you don't get much survival of seedlings even though they may germinate in October. Nature saves some of the hard seed for the next year, and there they will lie until a fine spring comes with rain and warm, sunny days, in proper sequence!

Once I heard there was an old pioneer house that after about fifty years was torn down and the lumber carted off. The next spring a precise square of glorious bluebonnets came up in that very area! Does the seed last fifty years? Or is that a folktale? It does last a long time, that I know. I wish I could have been there to see that very sight!

We once owned some land over in Llano County that sloped down to the Llano River and was dotted with huge, handsome live oak trees, very picturesque. In the spring, there was a succession of wildflowers, first a blanket of bluebonnets among the outcroppings of rock. It was a sight that fell gently on the eye. I remember once, when Lyndon was in the presidency, we were on a boat going leisurely down the Llano River, at twilight. The sun was setting behind Pack Saddle Mountain and the sky was a changing kaleidoscope. As we lay on top of the boat just listening to the sounds of spring with four or five congenial friends, the smell of bluebonnets, very like clover, wafted up to us and I thought, "How could I be happier than this?"

*Indian paintbrush is another favorite. The bluebonnet is infinitely more attractive to me when it is accented with Indian paintbrush (*Castilleja indivisa*). Vivid, orange red,* Castilleja *is named after a Spanish botanist, Domingo Castilleja.*

Indian paintbrush (*Castilleja* sp.), LBJ Ranch, Stonewall, Texas. JOSE AZEL, Contact Press Images

Texas bluebonnets *(Lupinus texensis),* National Wildflower Research Center. JOSE AZEL, Contact Press Images

Texas bluebonnets and red phlox *(Phlox drummondii),* Texas. JOHN SHAW

Indian paintbrush, LBJ Ranch, Texas. LARRY WEST

Indian paintbrush begins, like bluebonnet, in mid-March. The seeds need cold weather. It's wonderful when we have a very cold, wet winter, as we did before the spring of 1985. We had snow *twice! A cold, wet winter brings good germination, and then in early March in Texas the Indian paintbrush is spectacular, reaching its peak in mid-April and lasting all through April. The soil it likes best is sand and sandy loam.*

I remember sitting at my breakfast table with some friends from Washington, and there at the end of the runway, almost a quarter of a mile away, was this great orange-red flag of paintbrush! It was just a sight to make your spirits soar. And on the sides of the runway, particularly the east side, there was a long, brilliant line of them. I wish to goodness we knew better how to harvest their seed, because it is enormously expensive (about $95 for a quarter-pound) and very hard to find commercially.

One of the frustrating things about dealing with wildflowers is that so few species are harvested professionally, particularly in Texas, where they grow in such profusion. You can buy some species from California, some from Colorado, and some from North Carolina. Cheers for those who harvest the seeds, and a big salute!

Indian paintbrush grows throughout the Rockies, and I have come across it in Jackson Hole, Wyoming. I understand that there are a number of species in Eurasia.

Bluebonnets, or at least lupines, also have a very wide habitat; species of them exist all across the United States. I came upon some huge bushes of yellow lupines in California, growing in the median strips of highways. They were really more like shrubs than individual flowers. On the other side of the continent, when I was visiting Campobello, the summer home of President Roosevelt, there were—to my amazement—blue lupines!

*Another one of my favorites would have to be the gaillardia called Indian-blanket or fire wheel (*Gaillardia pulchella*). The reason I like it is because it is a survivor—hardy, drought-resistant, and it thrives in poor soil. I like masses of flowers, and gaillardia makes masses. A striking tapestry of color, it can cover several acres of pasture. Another reason I like it is because it is easy to grow. You plant gaillardia and you get gaillardia, which is not always the case with some of the more capricious, elusive flowers. I like, too, the variations in color.*

At the ranch we once planted some gaillardia seeds from another area. We planted them in rows to make a trial crop out of them. The flowers came in vast

Lady Bird Johnson standing in a field of Indian blanket, or firewheel *(Gaillardia pulchella).* JOSE AZEL

Mrs. Johnson seated among red phlox *(Phlox drummondii)* in front of the LBJ Ranch.
JOSE AZEL

profusion, but, alas, there was even more profusion in the leaves and stalks and stems! The colors of the flowers were different from what we knew, a lot of them were yellows and a lighter red. Right across the fence—there couldn't have been any difference in the soil, it seems to me, and certainly not in the weather and rainfall—were gaillardia planted by nature, or by us many years ago with just the hay-mulch method. The flowers were bright red, bright orange—not much foliage or stalk, shorter (indeed, quite a bit shorter) but more showy. I liked them better than the ones from bought seed. A similar flower, a close cousin, is Gaillardia aristata, *native from the Great Plains to the Pacific Northwest and south to Arizona and New Mexico. All were named for the French botanist Gaillard de Morentino.*

Have you ever played that after-dinner game "If you could find yourself seated next to anybody through history, living or dead, whom would you like to sit by?" I *would certainly choose, if not Lewis and Clark, one of the earliest botanists. The European botanists came over here in rather considerable numbers to explore this continent, to gather seeds and plants, and to take them back in those rocky little boats to their native England, France, or Spain. I would like to know some of the adventures they had and some of their thoughts when they suddenly came to the top of a hill and looked down on fifty acres of wildflowers in bloom!*

There is an Indian legend connected with every one of the flowers I know. There is also often some use to which the Indians put the roots or the blossoms for medicinal purposes. I wonder how many of those stories we—the Europeans—invented and how many are indeed Indian legends. The one about Indian-blanket is associated with an old Indian blanket-maker whose talent for weaving was known across the land. People would come from near and far to see his blankets, and maybe to try to trade for one. Finally, he made his last blanket for his own burial; it would be a gift to the Great Spirit. It was the prettiest one he had ever made, blending all his favorite browns, yellows, and reds into a beautiful pattern. He died, and was buried in the blanket. The Great Spirit was pleased because of the beauty of the gift, but he was also saddened because only those in the Happy Hunting Ground would be able to appreciate it. So, he decided to give this gift back to those whom the old Indian had left behind. The next year, above the grave, there bloomed a great profusion of flowers in all the colors and patterns of the Indian blanket, which spread and spread and bloomed forever.

*It would be impossible for me to talk about my favorite wildflowers without mentioning coreopsis (*Coreopsis tinctoria*). In the Texas Hill Country, it is a brilliant yellow with a sort of dark-brown, dubonnet center, and it grows on a slender, fragile stem with very little foliage, in masses—just a whole field of golden color.*

In the sequence of spring, coreopsis comes after bluebonnet and Indian paintbrush, and in some instances right along with Indian-blanket. I remember once we had a ranch called the Sharnhorst, where there was a lovely hill sloping down into a valley and in the distance an outcropping of pink granite. This hill was covered in April and on into May with golden coreopsis—just a vast, waving field of it. One day I was over there, and the wind was blowing and the grasses and the coreopsis were moving like the waves of the ocean! There were some horses in the field, a brown horse and a creamy white horse, and their tails and manes were waving. It was a sight to make one rejoice. I called it the golden hill. That spring a few weeks later, it rained again and that picture was repeated. It happened three times, the last time in the middle of June!

But if I had to choose what gives me the most pleasure, it would be a millefleurs *tapestry, a Persian carpet of many wildflowers spread before you when you gaze out on a roadside or a pasture and see every color in the rainbow. Bluebonnet or paintbrush or Indian-blanket may form the base, but others will be there: the yellow evening primrose (*Oenothera missourensis*) and the deep red-purple of the wine cups (*Callirhoe digitata*) and my almost-first favorite the delicate pale pink evening primrose (*Oenothera speciosa*). There will also be the tiny, white rock daisies (*Melampodium cinereum*) nestling close to the ground and then the tall, white spires of yucca—dozens of creamy white flowers on stalks that lift above the floor of wildflowers. There may be purple monarda spikes and then the pink and red and various shades of phlox. And, of course, purple verbena and a wealth of yellow flowers, names unknown to me and usually called by botanist friends—"a member of the* Compositae.*"*

In a good spring, I have seen Persian carpet roadsides stretching on for miles in front of me through pastures and meadows. Each one makes you gasp more than the one you just passed, and it will be the mixture of colors and the different heights that will give the most pleasure.

There are other flowers I do not remember having seen as part of the tapestry, which grow almost alone and have the most amazing habits. One is the white rain-lily

Wine-cups *(Callirhoe digitata),* Texas.
LARRY WEST

Pink evening primrose *(Oenothera speciosa),* Indian paintbrush (*Castilleja* sp.), and Texas bluebonnet *(Lupinus texensis),* Texas.
DAVID MUENCH

(Cooperia drummondii*), which I love. If it rains on Monday, particularly in April or May, on Tuesday afternoon, or maybe Wednesday morning, you will suddenly see, as if by magic, star-shaped white flowers on a slender stem—lilies with almost no foliage, which were not there yesterday! How do they grow twelve inches in twenty-four hours? Down in front of the ranch house, between the house and the Pedernales River, I have seen hundreds of these suddenly spring up like fairies in the night. If they grow in the granite soil close to some of the granite outcroppings, particularly in Llano County, they may be a sort of orange pink. In central Georgia, I have seen something very like it called the Atamasco-lily (*Zephyranthes atamasco*), only it is far bigger and more impressive, and likes being close to streambeds. It is absolutely splendid and grows in colonies, once more never mixed with other things.*

Our little rain-lily I have successfully transplanted from some parts of the river-front where no one ever goes except sometimes me. I have lifted the bulbs up gently with a trowel and brought them back and snuggled them in little groups close to the road where the most casual passerby can enjoy them.

Each season has its flowers that lift the heart.

*One of my favorite things to do is invite a botanist to the ranch for the day and go to see how many different species we can count in just fifteen minutes in a very short walk. On my runway at the LBJ Ranch there would be some basket flower (*Centaurea americana*), a pale lavender with fringed edges. Perhaps there would be large-flowered beard-tongue—also called false or wild foxglove (*Penstemon cobaea*)—fairly rare. And along the chalky cuts in late summer, probably a few globes of another favorite, mountain pink (*Centaurium beyrichii*), with delicate pink flowerets that grow from the size of a small baby fist to a large grapefruit. These mountain pinks, growing out of impossible-looking soil, are also called quinine weed, which the pioneers dried to make a tea to reduce fevers.*

*In almost any pasture there would also be the white prickly poppy (*Argemone albiflora*)—safe from cattle and even from people because it's too prickly to touch. I came across a pasture full of lush green grass, picturesque live oaks, black Angus cattle, and masses of white prickly poppies. I remember it as "my own Monet."*

Greenthread (*Thelesperma filifolium*) and prickly poppy (*Argemone polyanthemos*), Texas.
DAVID MUENCH

Wildflowers of Other Regions

Where Native Plants Grow

To appreciate the great diversity of plants native to the United States it is helpful to be aware of plant geography. Where plants live is a function of the way in which they live (physiology); their structure (morphology); how they associate with each other, with other organisms, and with geological factors (ecology); and how they change through time (evolve). Climate also is significant. As we travel about we are aware of how one part of the country looks different from another part. Upper New York State looks different from Connecticut, and Ohio looks different from both. Even parts of the same state may look different from other parts; Texas and California are large states, each with many parts that look different from other parts. Why do some parts look different from others? Because they *are* different. While the shapes of the land—hills, mountains, flatlands, marshes, deserts, coastlands—contribute to our awareness of differences, it is the kinds, distribution, and combinations of plants that influence us most. This is plant geography.

Henry Gleason and Arthur Cronquist recognize ten floristic provinces in North America: Tundra, Northern Conifer, Eastern Deciduous Forest, Coastal Plain, West Indian, Grassland, Cordilleran Forest, Great Basin, Californian, and Sonoran. These are designated in bold divisions on a map when, in reality, fingers and islands of each province intertwine and overlap where one meets another; the overall concept, however, helps us to understand why plants grow where they do. Because we are so accustomed to a state-by-state view, based on political boundaries rather than natural ones, this

Blue flag *(Iris versicolor)*, Maine. LES LINE

This map is derived from a similar map in Henry A. Gleason and Arthur Cronquist, The Natural Geography of Plants, *1964.* LIZ WAITE

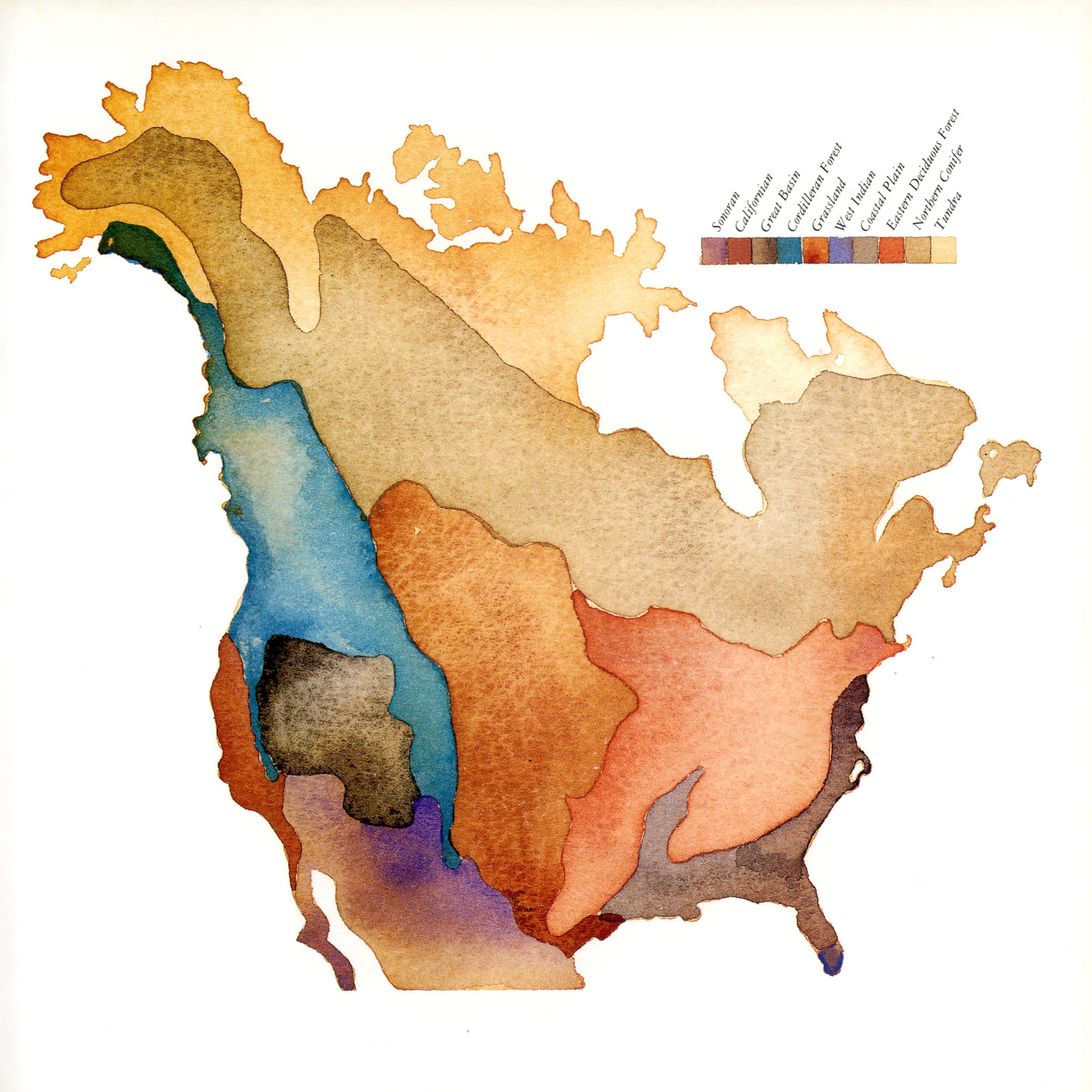
Sonoran
Californian
Great Basin
Cordilleran Forest
Grassland
West Indian
Coastal Plain
Eastern Deciduous Forest
Northern Conifer
Tundra

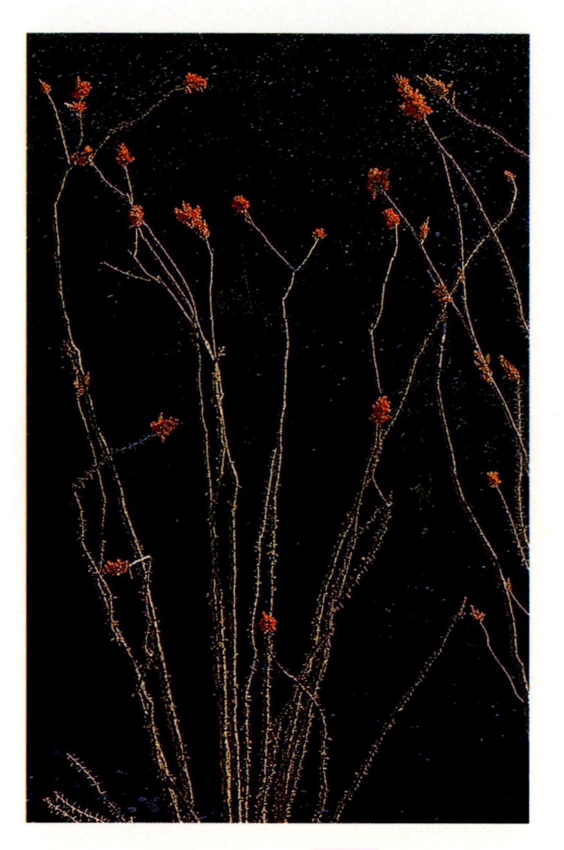

Ocotillo *(Fouquieria splendens)*, Texas. JIM BONES

ecological view of North America is an education in itself.

Some plants are restricted to extremely small ecological niches. Such is the case of many alpine and desert plants that through a long process of evolution have managed to survive in unusually harsh conditions. The devil's walking stick, or ocotillo (*Fouquieria splendens*), of the Sonoran Desert, for example, is drought-deciduous. Its leaves are discarded when their function is inhibited by lack of water. As soon as sufficient water is available, new leaves appear and photosynthesis resumes. Unlike northern deciduous trees that lose leaves and bear new ones only once each year, the ocotillo may grow and discard several sets throughout the year. The familiar house plant crown-of-thorns (*Euphorbia milii*) from Madagascar is similar to ocotillo and is adaptable to drought conditions. The Mexican palo verde (*Parkinsonia aculeata*) is so refined in its sensitivity to available water that in mildly dry periods it can drop the individual leaflets while retaining the central leaf stalk of each compound leaf. Seemingly leafless plants contain chlorophyll in the stems of the plant; photosynthesis that occurs within leaf tissues of most plants takes place within the stem tissues of cactus and other succulent plants. Although some of these have leaves, they are not always needed nor would they necessarily withstand the extreme and periodic dry conditions in which these plants grow. Alpine plants that grow in the stony rubble of high mountains often have deep roots that take up water from snow that melts higher on the mountain and flows downward under the stony surface. Some aquatic plants float, and some seashore plants withstand high tides of salt water that would kill or seriously damage other plants.

The ranges given for a particular species in wildflower books or guides are only indications in the broadest of terms. A species may be equally distributed throughout its range, it may be concentrated in one or more parts of the range and only sparsely represented on the fringes, or there may be concentrations or "islands" within the range with great distances between them.

Climatic Regions of America

Daylily *(Hemerocallis fulva),* Connecticut.
LES LINE

The United States Department of Agriculture, in its *Yearbook of Agriculture,* 1941, divides the United States into five climatic regions: the Humid East, the Subhumid Lands, the Great Plains, the Arid Region, and Summer-Dry Climates.

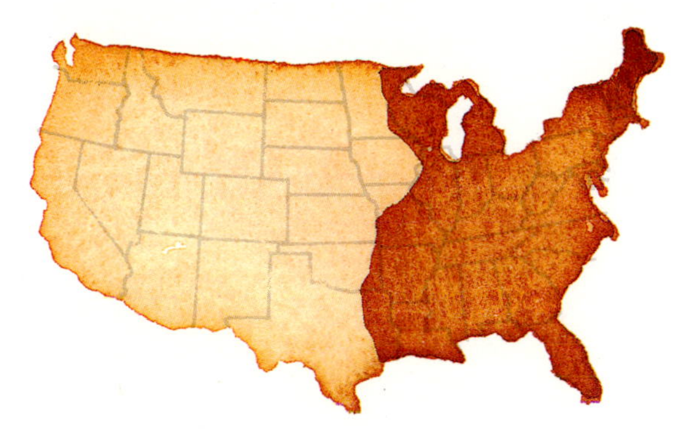

The Humid East

The Atlantic seaboard of America is only occasionally and in part influenced by its position on the ocean. Since the weather usually moves from west to east, most storm tracks pass from western Canada or the Rockies eastward by way of the Great Lakes. Much of the air that gets to the Atlantic coast passes over a wide stretch of land. Such continental air may be greatly chilled in winter or similarly heated in summer, so the eastern seaboard areas are subject to extremes of heat and cold similar to those of the interior, with interweaving periods tempered by ocean air or by warm air currents from the Caribbean. The Atlantic states have hotter summers and colder winters than western Europe. The climate of eastern America is also characterized by abrupt change from winter to summer, and with summer thunderstorms bearing rains more intense but of shorter duration than those of coastal Europe.

While recognizing the generally familiar nature of the weather in America, the European colonists became well aware of the differences. One of the earliest observations was by Captain John Smith, who likened the summers of Virginia to those of Spain but its winters to those of England, and commented, " . . . the like thunder and lightening to purefie the air, I have seldome either seene or heard in Europe." This was indeed a lustier land to which the settlers had come, a land of hotter summers and colder winters, of brighter and hotter sun and more tempestuous rains, a land suited to and provided with a greater variety of vegetation than the homelands of Europe. In one important respect only was the New World strikingly inferior to northwest Europe: the quality of the grasses. Almost none of the eastern American grasses withstood trampling and grazing. The annual grasses died off if heavily pastured because grazing prevented the setting of seed; the clovers and other herbaceous legumes so necessary to animal husbandry were vastly

Mountain rosebay *(Rhododendron catawbiense),* North Carolina. JIM BONES

New England aster *(Aster novae-angliae),* Maine. STEVE TERRILL

inferior to those of Europe because no heavy, herd-forming ungulates were native to eastern North America; hence native grasses and legumes did not accommodate trampling effects as a factor in their evolution.

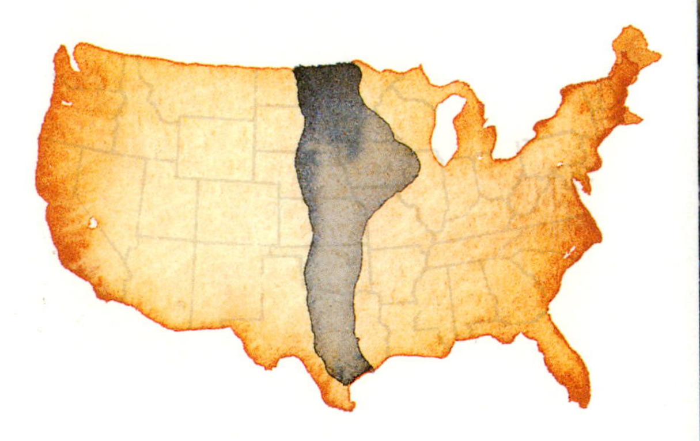

The Subhumid Lands

The interior subhumid lands of the United States are intermediate in climate as well as in position between the humid East and dry West. With this extensive belt of territory stretching from beyond the Canadian border to the Gulf of Mexico, annual precipitation exceeds potential evaporation but usually not by a very great margin. Generally, therefore, the climate of the subhumid lands errs (from an agricultural viewpoint) on the side of having too little precipitation and too many droughts rather than too much rainfall. The dryness increases from east to west. In a general way the interior subhumid lands are coincident with the prairies—the region of tall grasses—and only in central Illinois do extensive prairies extend eastward well beyond the subhumid region.

Prairie smoke *(Geum triflorum),* Minnesota.
R. HAMILTON SMITH

Gayfeather *(Liatris punctata),* Minnesota.
JIM BRANDENBURG

The earliest settlers surely must have thought that they had found paradise: for agriculture in no other region of the earth of equal size is so well endowed in surface configuration, soil, and climate. Drought is its one serious natural handicap. Never before had a people entered into such a "promised land," and never again will they be able to do so; no such frontiers remain. The occupying of the American prairies was an event of epochal significance for the nation and for the world. And for the immigrant plants, it became a paradise, too.

Mountain lady's slipper *(Cypripedium montanum),* Montana.
TOM AND PAT LEESON

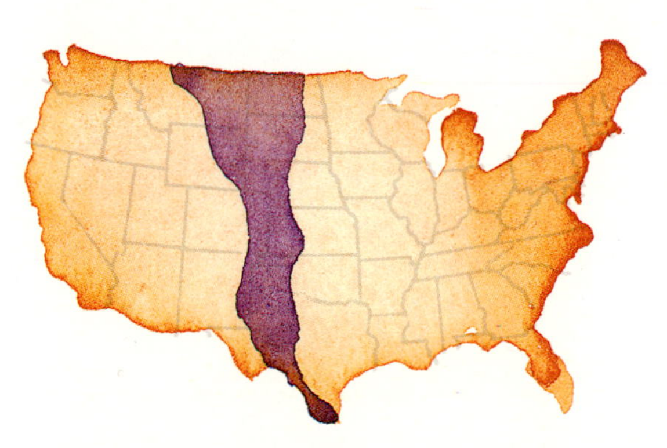

The Great Plains

The Great Plains, extending in a continuous belt 300 to 400 miles wide from Mexico into Canada, constitute the largest uninterrupted area with semiarid climate in North America. For the most part they are high plains ranging from 3,000 feet above sea level along their eastern margin to more than 4,000 feet where they meet the eastern slopes of the Rocky Mountains. Rainfall is scanty, averaging less than 20 inches annually except in the warmer southernmost portion, and only 10 inches in the north. The variability of the rainfall is great; almost everywhere the driest year brings less than 10 inches and the rainiest more than three times that amount.

In a desert, you know what to expect of the climate and plan accordingly. The same is true of the humid regions. But man has been misled by semiarid regions because they are sometimes humid, sometimes desert, and sometimes a cross between the two. Plants of foreign origin most adaptable to this region would be those from similar

Yucca (*Yucca* sp.), Texas.
DAVID MUENCH

parts of the world—particularly those of the eastern Mediterranean and Indo-Arabia—but it is necessary to recognize that this region was not settled by peoples from that part of the world; instead it was settled, except for the relatively small southern portion, by northern Europeans arriving by way of the East Coast. The plants they carried with them, intentionally and not, found this landscape much less similar to Europe than that of the eastern United States.

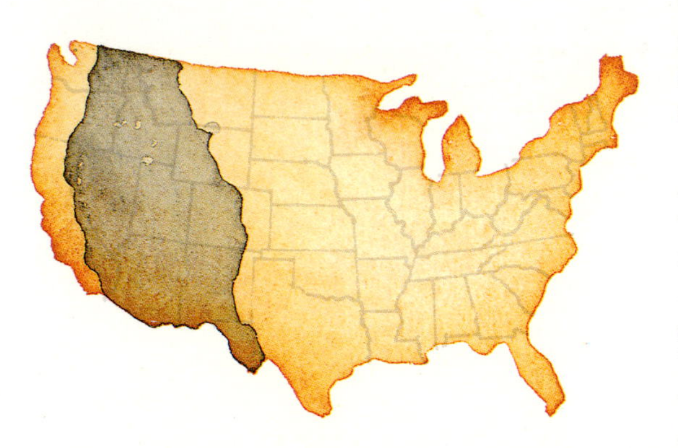

The Arid Region

The arid region can be divided into two major zones: southern—most of New Mexico, Arizona, and the southern part of California; and northern—the area between the Utah–Arizona line and the Canadian border. In the southern zone the summer winds sweep over the region from the south and are relatively moist, causing the period of maximum precipitation to coincide with the hottest months of the year, followed by very dry periods. In the mountains and higher plateaus to the north, however, there is a period of winter rain in addition to the wet summer period. Precipitation varies from a low of 3 inches in the Yuma area to 30 inches in the mountains of northern Arizona and New Mexico. Temperatures in general are very high, with great day-to-night fluctuations. The western portion is subject to prevailing westerly winds and receives its climatic characteristics from cyclonic storms sweeping in from the west. Here maximum precipitation comes in the winter and early spring months, varying from a low of about 4 inches in desert valleys west of Great Salt Lake to over 60 inches in the mountains of central Idaho and eastern Washington. The temperature extremes are typical of continental climates.

Gambling on the climate may be possible in semiarid regions, but for survival alone the dweller in an arid region must learn to respect the elements. He learns where water is, to husband it, to use just the right amount when needed, to protect watersheds. With skill, knowledge, and discipline, throughout history, man has created rich and verdant gardens in the desert. Nowhere in the United States has climate influenced the patterns of settlement and culture more definitively than in the arid regions of the West. Together with the topography and soils it determined rather rigidly the location of most settlement. The plants that are native to this region evolved in unique kinds of ways so that they could survive and function as a part of strikingly efficient systems that include mammals, insects, birds, and other forms of life. This was not a place for massive settlement and agriculture or for many plants from Europe to make new homes for themselves.

Ocotillo *(Fouquieria splendens)*, Arizona.
DAVID MUENCH

Paintbrush *(Castilleja* sp.*)* and lupine *(Lupinus* sp.*)*, Wyoming.
PAT O'HARA

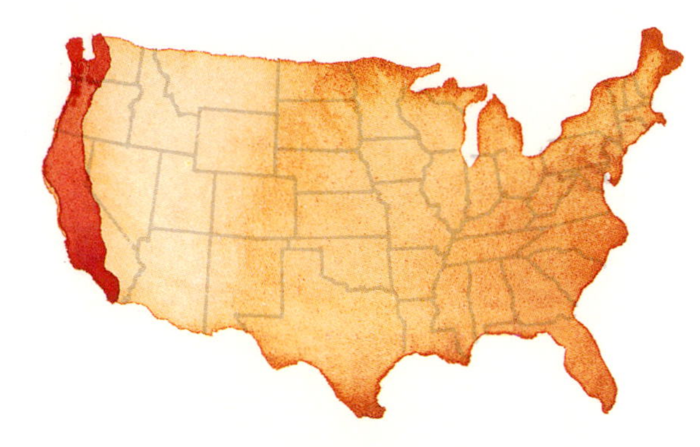

Summer-Dry Climates

The strip along the Pacific coast has a climate that in several ways reverses what occurs in all of the county to the east. A line drawn from the northeastern corner of Washington State through Lake Mead and extending south to the Mexican border passes through the driest parts of the United States. East of this line, precipitation falls mainly in summer; westward, toward the Pacific Ocean, in winter. From the Cascade and Sierra Nevada mountain ranges to the coast, except for interior valleys, the rainfall is sufficient to support a natural cover of grass, brush, and forest. In coastal mountains, where annual precipitation is from 40 to 100 inches, the heaviest forests of the United States grew and, in some places, grow still. The average annual rainfall along the coast ranges from about 10 inches in San Diego to over 80 inches at the entrance to the Strait of Juan de Fuca. A further prominent characteristic of Pacific coastal climates is mildness in winter and dryness in summer, a result of two influences: the presence of the Pacific Ocean to the west and the mountain barrier to the east. Air coming from the sea in winter is warmer than air chilled by passage over snow-covered land; the high and continuous wall of mountains acts as a mechanical check to air from the interior of the continent.

The plant introductions, immigrants, and escapes in this part of America are quite different from those eastward. Here are plants of Mediterranean origin, plants that grew along the roadsides of ancient Greece, Egypt, and Rome. They are not here simply because they found growing conditions similar to home but because the people who came were of Mediterranean origin, too. It was the Spaniards who moved into Mexico and then northward into southern Texas, New Mexico, and Arizona. But in California their missions extended northward to San Francisco. This was an easier land, one in which olives, citrus fruits, and bay and a multitude of familiar medicinal and other useful herbs, as well as garden and agricultural plants, could be grown. It was a land much like home. Here, too, vagabonds came along with seeds, supplies, equipment, and in the seams of missionary robes and sandals. The wild oats of California, which now cover hillsides, crowding out natives, is a Mediterranean weed, not just an escape from local agriculture. The two are not identical according to Edgar Anderson. Oats of agriculture and the weed-oats have different chromosome numbers; those of California are related to the weed-oats of the Mediterranean area and other parts of the Old World, and were familiar roadside plants in ancient Egypt and imperial Rome.

These agricultural climatic regions not only reveal clues about the distribution of introduced, immigrant, and escaped plants

but also suggest how very much the face of the landscape is the result of the particular time in history in which the massive settlement of the North American continent took place. The historic time determined what peoples from what parts of the earth came here. In the past, it could have been the Greeks, the Romans, the Egyptians, or the Chinese. Or, supposing the Spaniards had held on to California, Arizona, New Mexico —and even Texas—and had succeeded in penetrating northward into the arid region and, possibly the Great Plains, how much different would these landscapes be today?

Pink mountain heather (*Phyllodoce empetriformis*), Washington.
PAT O'HARA

Wildflowers Across America: A Regional Portfolio

Eastern Forest

151
Dwarf lake iris *(Iris lacustris)*, Michigan. LARRY WEST

152
Northern downy violet *(Viola fimbriatula)*, Michigan. LARRY WEST

153
Sweet white violet *(Viola blanda)*, Tennessee. LARRY WEST

Marsh blue violet *(Viola cucullata)*, Michigan. LARRY WEST

Stream violet *(Viola glabella)*, Washington. JOHN SHAW

Downy yellow violet *(Viola pubescens)*, Michigan. ROD PLANCK

Long-spurred violet *(Viola rostrata)*, Michigan. LARRY WEST

Canada violet *(Viola canadensis)*, Michigan. ROD PLANCK

154
Large-flowered trillium *(Trillium grandiflorum)*, Michigan. LARRY WEST

Large-flowered trillium, Michigan. LARRY WEST

Wake-robin *(Trillium erectum)*, New Brunswick. FREEMAN PATTERSON

Snow trillium *(Trillium nivale)*, Michigan. LARRY WEST

Wake-robin, Connecticut. LES LINE

Painted trillium *(Trillium undulatum)*, North Carolina. JOHN SHAW

155
Yellow trillium *(Trillium luteum)*, North Carolina. ROBERT P. CARR

156
False rue anemone *(Isopyrum biternatum)*, Michigan. JOHN SHAW

Wild geranium *(Geranium maculatum)*, Michigan. LARRY WEST

157
Rue anemone *(Anemonella thalictroides)*, Connecticut. LES LINE

Spring beauty *(Claytonia virginica)*, Michigan. JOHN SHAW

Starflower *(Trientalis borealis)*, Michigan. LARRY WEST

Round-lobed hepatica *(Hepatica americana)*, Michigan. LARRY WEST

Round-lobed hepatica, Michigan. ROD PLANCK

Round-lobed hepatica, Michigan. LES LINE

(continued on page 158)

Dwarf lake iris

Northern downy violet

Sweet white violet

Marsh blue violet

Stream violet

Downy yellow violet

Long-spurred violet

Canada violet

Large-flowered trillium

Large-flowered trillium

Wake-robin

Snow trillium

Wake-robin

Painted trillium

Yellow trillium

False rue anemone

Wild geranium

Rue anemone

Spring beauty

Starflower

Round-lobed hepatica

Round-lobed hepatica

Round-lobed hepatica

Solomon's seal

Trout-lily

158
Small Solomon's seal *(Polygonatum biflorum)*, North Carolina. SONJA BULLATY, ANGELO LOMEO

Trout-lily *(Erythronium americanum)*, Michigan. LES LINE

Spotted touch-me-not *(Impatiens capensis)*, Michigan. LARRY WEST

Trailing arbutus *(Epigaea repens)*, Michigan. LES LINE

159
Columbine *(Aquilegia canadensis)*, Massachusetts. LES LINE

Bloodroot *(Sanguinaria canadensis)*, Connecticut. LES LINE

Fireweed *(Epilobium angustifolium)*, Maine. LES LINE

False Solomon's seal *(Smilacina racemosa)*, Connecticut. LES LINE

Fire pink *(Silene virginica)*, North Carolina. SONJA BULLATY, ANGELO LOMEO

Wild oats *(Uvularia sessifolia)*, Michigan. LES LINE

Spotted touch-me-not

Trailing arbutus

Columbine

Bloodroot

Fireweed

False Solomon's seal

Fire pink

Wild oats

Naked miterwort

Jack-in-the-pulpit

160
Naked miterwort *(Mitella nuda)*, Michigan. LARRY WEST

Jack-in-the-pulpit *(Arisaema triphyllum)*, Michigan. ROD PLANCK

Wintergreen berries *(Gaultheria procumbens)*, Michigan. ROBERT P. CARR

Pine-sap *(Monotropa hypopithys)*, Michigan. LARRY WEST

Indian pipe *(Monotropa uniflora)*, Michigan. JOHN SHAW

Wintergreen berries

Pine-sap

Indian pipe

161
Twinflower *(Linnaea borealis),* Maine.
GLENN VAN NIMWEGEN

Foamflower *(Tiarella cordifolia),* North Carolina. PAT O'HARA

Bunchberry *(Cornus canadensis),* Michigan.
ROBERT P. CARR

Squirrel corn *(Dicentra canadensis),* Michigan.
ROD PLANCK

Gaywings *(Polygala paucifolia),* Michigan.
LARRY WEST

Twinflower

Foamflower

Bunchberry

Squirrel corn

Gaywings

Subtropical

163
Rose vervain *(Verbena tampensis),* Florida.
JAMES H. CARMICHAEL, JR.

164
Leopard lily *(Lilium catesbaei),* Florida.
MARGARETTE MEAD

165
Passionflower *(Passiflora incarnata),* Florida.
CONNIE TOOPS

Scarlet gilia *(Ipomopsis rubra),* Florida.
CONNIE TOOPS

Waterleaf *(Hydrolea corymbosa),* Florida.
JAMES H. CARMICHAEL, JR.

Blue curls *(Trichostema dichotomum),* Florida.
MARGARETTE MEAD

Swamp lily *(Crinum americanum),* Florida.
MARGARETTE MEAD

Coral bean *(Erythrina herbacea),* Florida.
JAMES H. CARMICHAEL, JR.

166
Pinelands ruellia *(Ruellia pinetorum),* Florida. CONNIE TOOPS

Bluebells *(Campanula floridana),* Florida.
JAMES H. CARMICHAEL, JR.

Seaside gentian *(Eustoma exaltatuim),* Florida.
JAMES H. CARMICHAEL, JR.

Butterfly pea *(Clitoria fragrans),* Florida.
MARGARETTE MEAD

167
Marsh pink *(Sabatia grandiflora),* Florida.
JAMES H. CARMICHAEL, JR.

Rose vervain

Leopard lily

Passionflower

Scarlet gilia

Waterleaf

Blue curls

Swamp lily

Coral bean

Pinelands ruellia

Bluebells

Seaside gentian

Butterfly pea

Marsh pink

Southwest

169
Claret cup *(Echinocereus triglochidiatus),* Texas.
DAVID MUENCH

170
Texas bluebonnets *(Lupinus texensis),* Texas.
DAVID MUENCH

171
Indian blanket *(Gaillardia pulchella),* and Texas buttercups *(Oenothera triloba),* Texas.
DAVID MUENCH

172
Plains blackfoot or Mountain daisy *(Melampodium Leucanthum),* Texas.
JIM BONES

173
Agave *(Agave havardiana),* Texas.
DAVID MUENCH

174
Texas bluebonnets *(Lupinus texensis)* and Indian paintbrush *(Castilleja indivisa),* Texas. DAVID MUENCH

175
Arkansas yucca *(Yucca arkansana)* and wild buckwheat *(Erigonum sp.),* Texas.
DAVID MUENCH

Coreopsis *(Coreopsis tinctoria),* Texas.
JIM BONES

Red phlox *(Phlox drummondii),* and paintbrush *(Castilleja sp.),* Texas. JIM BONES

Texas bluebonnets, wine-cups *(Callirhoe digitata),* and evening primrose *(Oenothera missouriensis),* Texas.
JIM BONES

176
Crimson sage *(Salvia henryi),* Texas.
JIM BONES

Lace cactus (*Echinocereus* sp.), Texas. JIM BONES

177
Blind prickly-pear *(Opuntia rufida),* Texas.
DAVID MUENCH

Claret cup

Plains blackfoot or Mountain daisy

Rock-nettle

Agave

Crimson sage

Lace cactus

Blind prickly-pear

Fields, Meadows, Prairies

179

Field of mustard (*Brassica* sp.), Washington.
PAT O'HARA/DRK

180

Wild flax *(Linum lewisii)* and mustard (*Brassica* spp.), North Dakota,
JIM BRANDENBURG

Tidy tips *(Layia platyglossa),* California.
MARY ELLEN SCHULTZ

Common fleabane *(Erigeron philadelphicus),* Connecticut. LES LINE

Compass plant *(Silphium laciniatum),* Minnesota.
JIM BRANDENBURG

Daisy fleabane *(Erigeron annuus),* New York.
LES LINE

181

Arnica *(Arnica mollis),* Oregon. STEVE TERRILL

182

Prostrate bluets *(Houstonia serpyllifolia),* North Carolina.
JOHN SHAW

183

Blue-eyed grass *(Sisyrinchium montanum),* New Brunswick.
FREEMAN PATTERSON

Dame's rocket *(Hesperis matronalis),* Connecticut. LES LINE

Fringed gentian *(Gentiana crinita),* Connecticut. LES LINE

Deptford pink *(Dianthus armeria),* Michigan.
LARRY WEST

Yellow goatsbeard (*Tragopogon dubius*), Minnesota.
R. HAMILTON SMITH

Wild sweet William *(Phlox maculata),* New York. LES LINE

(Continued on page 185)

Field of mustard

Wild flax and mustard

Tidy tips

Common fleabane

Compass plant

Daisy fleabane

Arnica

Prostrate bluets

Blue-eyed grass

Dame's rocket

Fringed gentian

Deptford pink

Yellow goatsbeard

Wild sweet William

Butter-and-eggs

Larkspur

Moth mullein

Winter cress

Gayfeather

Birdsfoot trefoil

184
Butter-and-eggs *(Linaria vulgaris)*, Michigan. LES LINE

Larkspur *(Delphinium* sp.*)*, California. MARY ELLEN SCHULTZ

Moth mullein *(Verbascum blattaria)*, Michigan. LARRY WEST

Winter cress *(Barbarea vulgaris)*, New York. LES LINE

Gayfeather *(Liatris* sp.*)* and monarch butterfly, Minnesota. JIM BRANDENBURG

Birdsfoot trefoil *(Lotus corniculatus)*, Connecticut. LES LINE

185
Goldenrod *(Solidago* sp.*)*, Michigan. ROBERT P. CARR

Goldenrod

Ragged robin

Michigan lily

Wild bergamot

Canada lily

Bird's-eye primrose

186
Ragged robin *(Lychnis flos-cuculi),* Connecticut. LES LINE

Michigan lily *(Lilium michiganense),* Michigan. JOHN SHAW

Wild bergamot *(Monarda fistulosa),* Michigan. ROD PLANCK

Canada lily *(Lilium canadense),* Connecticut. LES LINE

Bird's-eye primrose *(Primula mistassinica),* Michigan. JOHN GERLACH/DRK

187
Harvest brodiaea *(Brodiaea elegans),* California. PAT O'HARA

Harvest brodiaea

Spotted knapweed

Canada thistle

Field of spotted knapweed

Northern blazing star

Pitcher's thistle

188
Spotted knapweed *(Centaurea maculosa)*, Connecticut. LES LINE
Canada thistle *(Cirsium arvense)*, Michigan. JOHN SHAW
Field of spotted knapweed, Michigan. LARRY WEST
Northern blazing star *(Liatris borealis)*, Michigan. JOHN GERLACH/DRK
Pitcher's thistle *(Cirsium pitcheri)*, Michigan. ROD PLANCK

189
Wild teasel *(Dipsacus sylvestris)*, Michigan. LARRY WEST
Wild bergamot *(Monarda fistulosa)*, Connecticut. LES LINE

Wild teasel

Wild bergamot

Checkers

Shrubby cinquefoil

Thistle sage

Baby blue eyes

Butterflyweed

Mountain pasque flower

190
Checkers (*Sidalcea* sp.), California.
DAVID CAVAGNARO/DRK
Shrubby cinquefoil (*Potentilla fruticosa*), Minnesota. JOHN SHAW
Thistle sage (*Salvia carduacea*), California.
MARY ELLEN SCHULTZ
Baby blue eyes (*Nemophila menziesii*), California. JEFF FOOTT/DRK
Butterflyweed (*Asclepias tuberosa*), Michigan.
LARRY WEST
Mountain pasque flower (*Anemone occidentalis*), Colorado.
TOM AND PAT LEESON

191
Prairie smoke (*Geum triflorum*).
R. HAMILTON SMITH
Pasque flower (*Anemone patens*).
R. HAMILTON SMITH

Prairie smoke

Pasque flower

Wet Places

193
Fragrant water lily *(Nymphaea odorata),* Maine. JOHN SHAW

194
Cobra plant *(Darlingtonia californica),* California. LES LINE

Cobra plant detail, California. LES LINE

Skunk cabbage *(Symplocarpus foetidus),* Michigan. LES LINE

Pitcher plant leaf *(Sarracenia purpurea),* Michigan. LARRY WEST

Pitcher plant flower, Michigan. LARRY WEST

195
Yellow skunk cabbage *(Lysichitum americanum),* Oregon. DAVID MUENCH

196
Seashore mallow *(Kosteletzkya virginica),* North Carolina. LES LINE

Bullhead lily *(Nuphar variegatum),* Maine. LES LINE

197
Indian pond lily *(Nuphar polysepala),* Oregon. STEVE TERRILL

198
Marsh marigold *(Caltha palustris),* Michigan. ROBERT P. CARR

Marsh marigold, New York. LES LINE

199
Elkslip *(Caltha leptosepala),* and corn-lily *(Veratrum californicum),* Colorado. JIM BONES

200
Iris *(Iris missouriensis),* New Mexico. JIM BONES

201
Blue water lily *(Nymphaea elegans),* Florida. JAMES H. CARMICHAEL, JR.

Common cattail *(Typha latifolia),* Maine. LES LINE

Swamp lily *(Crinum americanum),* Florida. LARRY WEST

Lizard's-tail *(Saururus cernuus),* Louisiana. LARRY WEST

Hollow-stemmed Joe-Pye-weed *(Eupatorium fistulosum),* Connecticut. LES LINE

Pickerelweed *(Pontederia cordata),* Florida. MARGARETTE MEAD

Fragrant water lily

Cobra plant

Cobra plant detail

Skunk cabbage

Pitcher plant leaf

Pitcher plant flower

Yellow skunk cabbage

Seashore mallow

Bullhead lily

Indian pond lily

Marsh marigold

Marsh marigold

Elkslip and corn-lily

Iris

Blue water lily

Common cattail

Swamp lily

Lizard's-tail

Hollow Joe-Pye-weed

Pickerelweed

Arid Lands

203
Mexican poppy *(Eschscholzia mexicana),* Arizona.
DAVID MUENCH

204
Yellow rock-nettle *(Eucnide bartonioides),* Texas. ROBERT P. CARR

205
Phacelia *(Phacelia calthifolia),* California.
BILL RATCLIFFE

Sego lily *(Calochortus nuttalli),* Utah.
BILL RATCLIFFE

206
Barrel cactus (*Ferocactus viridescens*), California.
PAT O'HARA

Barrel cactus (*Ferocactus wislizeni*), Arizona.
DAVID MUENCH

207
Beavertail cactus *(Opuntia basilaris),* California. PAT O'HARA

208
Rock-nettle *(Eucnide urens),* California.
PAT O'HARA

209
Calico cactus (*Echinocereus engelmannii*), California. ROD PLANCK

Fishhook cactus (*Mamillaria dioica*), California. PAT O'HARA

Yellow pitaya (*Echinocereus dasyacanthus*), Texas.
ROBERT P. CARR

210
Desert primrose *(Oenothera brevipes),* Nevada. PAT O'HARA

Indian apple *(Datura discolor),* Arizona.
R. HAMILTON SMITH

Globe mallow *(Sphaeralcea angustifolia),* Utah.
GLENN VAN NIMWEGEN

Desert fivespot *(Malvastrum rotundifolium),* California. PAT O'HARA

Blue-curls *(Phacelia* sp.*),* California.
PAT O'HARA

Mohave aster *(Machaeranthera tortifolia),* California.
STEPHEN J. KRASEMANN

211
Yellow bee-plant *(Cleome lutea),* Oregon.
STEVE TERRILL

Mexican poppy

Yellow rock-nettle

Phacelia

Sego lily

Barrel cactus

Barrel cactus

Beavertail cactus

Rock-nettle

Calico cactus

Fishhook cactus

Yellow pitaya

Desert primrose

Indian apple

Globe mallow

Desert fivespot

Blue-curls

Mohave aster

Yellow bee-plant

Birdcage evening primrose

212
Birdcage evening primrose *(Oenothera deltoides),* Oregon.
STEVE TERRILL

213
Birdcage evening primrose, Arizona.
DAVID MUENCH

Birdcage evening primrose

Orchids

215
Grass pink *(Calopogon pulchellus)* and yellow trumpet *(Sarracenia alata)*, Texas.
JIM BONES

216
Butterfly orchid *(Epidendrum tampense)* and crab spider, Florida.
MARGARETTE MEAD

Ghost orchid *(Polyrrhiza lindenii)*, Florida.
M. P. KAHL/DRK

Showy orchid *(Orchis spectabilis)*, North Carolina.
ROBERT P. CARR

Leafless beaked orchid *(Stenorhynchus orchiodes)* and lubber grasshopper, Florida. JAMES H. CARMICHAEL, JR.

Early coralroot *(Corallorhiza trifida)*, Minnesota.
JIM BRANDENBURG

Clam shell orchid *(Epidendrum cochleatum)*, Florida. LARRY WEST

217
Spotted coralroot *(Corallorhiza maculata)*, Minnesota.
JIM BRANDENBURG

Striped coralroot *(Corallorhiza striata)*, Michigan. ROD PLANCK

218
Arethusa *(Arethusa bulbosa)* and pale laurel *(Kalmia pollifolia)*, Maine. DAVID MUENCH

219
Grass pink *(Calopogon pulchellus)*, Michigan.
JOHN SHAW

White fringed orchid *(Habenaria blephariglottis)*, Michigan. LARRY WEST

Rose pogonia *(Pogonia ophioglossoides)*, Michigan.
JOHN GERLACH/DRK

Yellow fringed orchid *(Habenaria ciliaris)*, North Carolina.
MARGARETTE MEAD

Purple fringed orchid *(Habenaria psycodes)*, Michigan. LARRY WEST

Ragged fringed orchid *(Habenaria lacera)*, Michigan. ROD PLANCK

220
Fairy slipper *(Calypso bulbosa)*, New Brunswick.
FREEMAN PATTERSON

White lady's-slipper *(Cypripedium candidum)*, Minnesota.
JIM BRANDENBURG

Pink lady's-slipper *(Cypripedium acaule)*, Minnesota.
JIM BRANDENBURG

Yellow lady's-slipper *(Cypripedium calceolus)*, Michigan. LARRY WEST

Showy lady's-slipper *(Cypripedium reginae)*, Michigan. ROD PLANCK

Pink lady's-slipper, white form, New Brunswick. LES LINE

221
Ram's-head lady's-slipper *(Cypripedium arietinum)*, Michigan.
ROD PLANCK

Pink lady's-slipper *(Cypripedium acaule)*, Connecticut. LES LINE

Grass pink and yellow trumpet

Butterfly orchid and crab spider

Ghost orchid

Showy orchid

Leafless beaked orchid and lubber grasshopper

Early coralroot

Clamshell orchid

Spotted coralroot

Striped coralroot

Arethusa and pale laurel

Grass pink

White fringed orchid

Rose pogonia

Yellow fringed orchid

Purple fringed orchid

Ragged fringed orchid

Fairy slipper

White lady's-slipper

Pink lady's-slipper

Yellow lady's-slipper

Showy lady's-slipper

Pink lady's-slipper, white form

Ram's-head lady's-slipper

Pink lady's-slipper

Rocky Mountains

223
Paintbrush (*Castilleja rhexifolia*) and knotweed (*Puliginam bistortoides*), Colorado. DAVID MUENCH

224
Parry primrose *(Primula parryi)*, Utah. PAT O'HARA

225
Elk thistle *(Cirsium foliosum)*, Wyoming. PAT O'HARA

226
Blue columbine *(Aquilegia caerulea)*, Colorado. DAVID MUENCH

227
Yellow columbine *(Aquilegia chrysantha)*, Utah. STEPHEN J. KRASEMANN/DRK

Blue columbine *(Aquilegia caerulea)*, Wyoming. PAT O'HARA/DRK

Yellow columbine *(Aquilegia chrysantha)*, Utah. GLENN VAN NIMWEGEN

228
Owl's clover *(Orthocarpus* sp.) and paintbrush *(Castilleja rhexifolia)*, Colorado. DAVID MUENCH

229
Penstemon (*Penstemon* sp.), Colorado. Steve Terrill

230
Glacier lily *(Erythronium grandiflorum)*, Colorado. LES LINE

Harebell *(Campanula rotundifolia)*, Wyoming. PAT O'HARA

Shootingstar *(Dodecatheon pauciflorum)*, Colorado. LARRY WEST

Brodiaea (*Brodiaea capitata*), California. PAT O'HARA

Globeflower *(Trollius laxus)*, Wyoming. PAT O'HARA

Monkshood *(Aconitum columbianum)*, Montana. PAT O'HARA

231
Star tulip *(Calochortus nudus)*, California. LES LINE

Western fringed gentian *(Gentiana dentosa)*, Wyoming. PAT O'HARA

Alpine bluebells *(Mertensia alpina)*, Colorado. LES LINE

Sneezeweed (*Hymenoxys* sp.), Colorado. LARRY ULRICH/DRK

Paintbrush and Knotweed

Parry primrose

Elk thistle

Blue columbine

Yellow columbine

Blue columbine

Yellow columbine

Owl's clover and Indian paintbrush

Penstemon

Glacier lily

Harebell

Shootingstar

Brodiaea

Globeflower

Monkshood

Star tulip

Western fringed gentian

Alpine bluebells

Sneezeweed

Pacific Northwest

233
Storksbill *(Erodium cicutarium)* and cottonwood seeds, Oregon. STEVE TERRILL

234
Dame's rocket *(Hesperis matronalis)* and columbine *(Aquilegia exima),* Oregon. STEVE TERRILL

235
White-rayed mule's ears *(Wyethia amplexicaulis),* Oregon. STEVE TERRILL

236
Penstemon *(Penstemon sp.),* Washington. STEVE TERRILL

237
Penstemon *(Penstemon davidsonii)* and parnassian butterfly, Washington. STEVE TERRILL

238
Monkeyflowers *(Mimulus* sp.*),* Oregon. STEVE TERRILL

239
Flett violets *(Viola flettii),* Washington. PAT O'HARA/DRK

240
Phlox *(Phlox speciosa),* Oregon. STEVE TERRILL
Lupine *(Lupinus sp.),* Oregon. STEVE TERRILL,

241
Lupine, Washington. PAT O'HARA

242
Buttercup (*Ranunculus scleratus*), Oregon, STEVE TERRILL

243
Rabbit brush *(Chrysothamnus nauseosus),* Crater Lake, Oregon. STEVE TERRILL

244
Salal *(Gaultheria shallon),* Washington. TOM AND PAT LEESON
Bitter root *(Lewisia rediviva),* Oregon. PAT O'HARA
Grass widows *(Sisyrinchium douglasii)* Washington. PAT O'HARA
Old-man-of-the-mountains *(Anemone occidentalis),* Washington. PAT O'HARA

245
Foxglove *(Digitalis purpurea),* Washington. STEVE TERRILL

Redstem storksbill and cottonwood seeds

Dame's rocket and columbine

White-rayed mule's ears

Penstemon

Penstemon and parnassian butterfly

Monkeyflowers

Flett violets

Phlox

Lupine

Lupine

Buttercups

Rabbit brush

Salal

Bitter root

Grass widows

Old-man-of-the-mountains

Foxglove

High Arctic

247
Alaska blue anemone *(Anemone multiceps),* Alaska. STEPHEN J. KRASEMANN/DRK

248
Arctic poppy *(Papaver radicatum),* Yukon. J. A. KRAULIS

Dwarf fireweed *(Epilobium latifolium),* Ellesmere Island. STEPHEN J. KRASEMANN/DRK

Dwarf fireweed (*Epilobium* sp.), Yukon. J.A. KRAULIS

Mountain heather *(Cassiope tetragona),* Ellesmere Island. STEPHEN J. KRASEMANN/DRK

249
Northern primrose *(Primula borealis)* and western buttercup *(Ranunculus occidentalis),* Alaska. DAVID CAVAGNARO/DRK

250
Blackish oxytrope *(Oxytropis nigrescens),* Alaska. STEPHEN J. KRASEMANN/DRK

Bog rosemary *(Andromeda pollifolia),* Alaska. DAVID CAVAGNARO/DRK

252
Woolly lousewort *(Pedicularis lanata),* Baffin Island. STEPHEN J. KRASEMANN/DRK

Arctic forget-me-not *(Eritricium aretoides),* Alaska. LES LINE

253
Northern Jacob's ladder *(Polemonium boreale),* Alaska. LES LINE

Lapland rosebay *(Rhododendron lapponicum),* Alaska. STEPHEN J. KRASEMANN/DRK

Diapensia *(Diapensia lapponica),* Mount Washington, New Hampshire. ROBERT P. CARR

Mountain avens (*Dryas integrifolia*), Baffin Island. STEPHEN J. KRASEMANN/DRK

254
Alaskan spring beauty *(Claytonia sarmentosa),* Alaska. STEPHEN J. KRASEMANN/DRK

255
Purple mountain saxifrage *(Saxifraga oppositifolia),* Canada. STEPHEN J. KRASEMANN/DRK

Alaska blue anemone

Arctic poppy

Dwarf fireweed

Dwarf fireweed

Mountain heather

Northern primrose and western buttercup

Blackish oxytrope

Bog rosemary

Woolly lousewort

Arctic forget-me-not

Northern Jacob's ladder

Lapland rosebay

Diapensia

Mountain avens

Alaskan spring beauty

Purple mountain saxifrage

In New Landscapes: Wildflowers Tamed

The Beautification Movement and Highway Legislation

Claret cup cactus *(Echinocereus triglochidiatus),* Arizona. DAVID MUENCH

Lady Bird Johnson, flanked by Secretary of the Interior Stewart Udall and Laurance Rockefeller, at a White House luncheon on April 27, 1967.

Many memories overflow from my brief but yeasty time on the national stage—a mixture of shovels and ceremonial plantings, of speech-cards and interviews, adventures down the Snake River and the Rio Grande, and meetings that stretched from the White House to national highway associations to local garden clubs. I recall the cold January day when our family's gift to the White House, a children's garden, was dedicated; the "star" of the occasion, our grandson Lyn, walked straight into the fish pond! And the day when a host of governors' wives came to plant fifty-four flowering dogwoods on Gravelly Point, a stretch of land across from National Airport. It had been orchestrated that all of us would throw in the last spadeful of dirt simultaneously—a wonderful photo opportunity for the press. We were to be accompanied by a fanfare from the band while state flags fluttered colorfully in the sky. However, as it turned out, the trees were located as much as two blocks apart. We walked through mud up to our shoe tops in 29-degree weather in a biting wind that churned up whitecaps on the Potomac—so much for precision planning! I think of dear Mary Lasker. It was she who pointed out to me that Lyndon's 1965 State of the Union Message was the first time any leader used the word beauty *in a national address, and he was the first president to call for beautification of the country as part of his program.*

There was so much that called out to be done. The first tentative steps were taken on a wintry afternoon in 1964 at the LBJ Ranch after the recent election victory. Secretary of the Interior Stewart Udall, who came to confer with Lyndon, also set aside

some time for me. We discussed the role I might play as First Lady to strengthen the cause of conservation. From our visit evolved a plan of paying tribute to citizen accomplishment, of creating a hometown action committee to give form to ideas and to try its hand at the elusive art of making things happen. It was here that the idea of the Committee for a More Beautiful Capital was born.

This was strictly a volunteer group, operating without bylaws or organization chart, and we decided to meet monthly at the White House. We agreed that our best course of action was to work on becoming a rallying point for everything from more litter receptacles to the design of federal buildings.

In May of 1965, a two-day White House Conference on Natural Beauty was held, chaired by Laurance Rockefeller, and approximately 115 panelists who had proved their ability and experience in business, industry, labor, public service, and citizen action were invited to participate. By 1967 more than two thirds of the nation's governors had convened similar conferences on natural beauty. From these sprang a great many impressive local beautification efforts.

From the business community, an increasing number of "believers" emerged. Beautification and tourism made for profitable commerce, and in a great many states a sizable income stemmed from the tourist industry. Flower shows, wildflower trails, restoration projects, and magnificent gardens attracted visitors. My own interest in "beautification" went hand in hand with the See America movement. Frequently my trips focused attention on both programs.

From those beginnings our efforts spread to other parts of the country. Beautification has a ripple-wave effect; it is contagious. Millions of citizens get involved: engineers who have a social concern beyond mere technical skill, editors who know a crusade against ugliness is worthy of page-one attention, aroused city planners and activists, poets and artists of the landscape, officeholders and attorneys.

Secretary Udall said: "What we are really doing here is showing other people what can be done. The program we are all concerned about—the design of the country, its beauty, the right arrangement of what man does and what nature has already done, and would like to do if you give it a chance—this has to permeate government. It has to permeate ultimately the business community. It has to become part of our way of life."

(Top left) President Lyndon B. Johnson, on October 2, 1968, signing the following bills into law: National Wild Rivers System, National System of Trails, North Cascades National Park, and Redwoods National Park. Among the witnesses are Mrs. Johnson, Secretary Udall, Chief Justice Earl Warren, and Senator Henry Jackson. (Top right) Lady Bird Johnson viewing plantings in Washington, D.C., on March 30, 1968, with Nash Castro, future president of the National Wildflower Research Center.

(Bottom left) Lady Bird Johnson planting a tree with Mary Lasker, while on a bus tour of beautification areas in Washington, D.C. (Bottom right) Mrs. Johnson at the January 19, 1969, dedication of the White House Children's Garden, with daughter Lynda and granddaughter Lucinda. JACK KIGHTLINGER

When we were asked by other communities, "What can we do?" the suggested improvements were legion: plant colonnades of trees to line the streets, and place tubs of flowers throughout the city; use simple and excellent designs for informational signs; reinstall overhead wires underground; set out hundreds of handsome benches and litter receptacles; create pedestrian streets around plazas and shopping areas; use minibuses to facilitate downtown traffic circulation; make waterfront parks for popular enjoyment—all of these ideas are ingredients that can transform cities into places of warmth and welcome for workers, for shoppers, and for tourists.

We urged that each community define the problems that plagued it and work together to correct them. Although government could be helpful in some situations, positive local solutions to correct local ills would provide the best long-term results. Businesses, large and small, that undertook landscaping projects, or paint and restoration, or the screening of parking lots with trees and attractive plantings, found themselves with increased goodwill and gratitude, and often more customers. I can remember businessmen like IBM chairman Tom Watson telling me how it had paid off to landscape new manufacturing plants distinctively and to be a visible plus in a town.

In one southern community, a bank paid for a mile of landscaping at the city's entrance. The banker told me that no billboard, no radio or television advertising campaign had ever won him the daily applause he received for this project from his customers. The bank was in the process of trying to get permission from the city to let it do the same thing at the city's three other entrances. So many city fringes present the worst face of the town, a hodgepodge and a scrabble of flashing signs. I remember thinking that the green entrance to that community said "Welcome" to me.

Will Rogers once remarked that the two towns in America with the most personality were New Orleans and San Antonio. Today both towns enjoy a booming tourist trade. At various points in their past, they refused to let their personalities be devoured by the onslaught of so-called progress—the metro dollars increased as a result. Commerce capitalized on the natural gift of waterfronts and the natural heritage of many bloodlines. At Hemisfair in San Antonio, the planners built a great, modern exposition area, but thirty old buildings nearby were lovingly preserved and restored, and they are among the most colorful punctuation marks at the complex.

Among American cities are many examples of what can happen with imagi-

Lady Bird Johnson with Secretary Stewart Udall on April 2, 1969, at Big Bend National Park on a Trails Through Texas trip.
ROBERT KNUDSEN

native planning. For instance, Philadelphia found a way to depress its new Delaware River Expressway and put a pedestrian plaza on top to bind the city to its waterfront. It makes a statement that "People matter, not just traffic." Ghirardelli Square in San Francisco is a marvel of attractions and surprises for the strolling shopper. Niccolet Mall in Minneapolis is an inviting, lively commercial area built to make shopping a pleasure.

There were a great many rebuilding projects undertaken in our country in the sixties—not just in the old terms of freeways ripping through established neighborhoods and parks, or of drab public housing so all-alike that it reminded one of Gertrude Stein's phrase "There's no there there.*" The challenge was not whether to build, but how to do it with beauty and a passion for life and its fulfillment. The environment is where we all meet; where we all have a mutual interest; it is one thing that all of us share. Whatever its condition, it is, after all, a reflection of ourselves—our tastes, our aspirations, our successes, and our failures. Fortunately, if we want to badly enough, we can do much to change what is not pleasurable to the eye and spirit. Even in the poorest neighborhoods you can find a geranium in a coffee can, a window box set against the scaling side of a tenement, a border of roses struggling to live in a tiny patch of open ground. Where flowers bloom, so does hope.*

Green oases and neighborhood parks within cities offer a promise. If people in humdrum jobs, in drab buildings, surrounded by noise and confusion, know they can move out of all that into areas of serene beauty and quiet, even for a brief time each day, they can better cope with conditions that may bring them to the breaking point. I recall my shock when I learned that 70 *percent of the people in our country lived on* 1 *percent of the land. The need to find release from the tensions of city life is crucial.*

Concern for the whole environment, attention to the human scale, and an emphasis upon areas of natural beauty, both inside the city and beyond its borders, were essential to what we were trying to accomplish and encourage. The twentieth-century citizen, no less than his ancestor in another age, craves and needs to be reminded of his place in nature. The park and the public garden, the shady forest trail, the tree-lined river winding through a city—these are not only physical but spiritual resources.

During Lyndon's administration some 278 *significant conservation and beautification measures were enacted—fifty of them he thought could be termed "major."*

Mule's ears *(Wyethia amplexicaulis)* and sticky geranium *(Geranium viscosissimum)*, Wyoming.
DAVID MUENCH

They included securing more than one million additional acres for our National Park System, nearly 200 miles of national seashore, a system of urban and rural trails, including the Pacific Coast Trail from Mexico to Canada, and the establishment of a National Wild and Scenic Rivers System.

In my own experience, nature was encountered most intimately when I left the city to go to our ranch. Once there, I quickly fell in tune with the great rhythms of life. I knew whether the sky held a new moon or a full moon or the dark of the moon. When storms came I thrilled to the crackle of lightning and the majesty of thunder. I rediscovered a sense of hearing, and a sense of smell from the perfume of blossoms and grasses after a rain. This participation in the seasons and the weather is one of the most vital and renewing experiences of life—too important to be reserved for vacations or for the few.

One spring, I took a trip down into Virginia. For a short segment of the journey we drove along Highway No. 1, with its jumble of signs and junkyards—the landscape blighted. And then we swung over to Interstate 95 as it swept up the rolling hills between tall stands of oaks and evergreens laced with white dogwoods. From the road itself, you could understand why Virginians love their state. Like them, we all recognize the difference between the road that beckons and the road that depresses. I know what a lift of spirit and surge of pride I feel when I drive up over the crest of the hills at home near Llano, Texas. There, in the distance is Pack Saddle Mountain, and on either side of the broad right-of-way a long sweep of bluebonnets in the spring and then a roadside park, golden with daisylike wildflowers and picnic tables under the live oaks.

In the kaleidoscope of my most cherished memories is a road through Vermont in early October when on the majestic mountains the maples were flaming torches of scarlet and crimson against the evergreens. Asters and goldenrod lined the roadside, and nature's bounty of pumpkins and apples was piled high on roadside stands. Merritt Parkway in Connecticut is another of the most enchanting natural gardens in the world. Along the Pacific Coast, the first designated Scenic Highway in the nation is a dramatic road that hugs the jagged cliffs above the surf and winds its way from Carmel, California, to the Hearst San Simeon Castle. These great roads not only get you from here to there, they afford a revelation of America's great beauty along the way.

Congress passed the Highway Beautification Act in 1965, legislation that offered the hope of many more public decisions in behalf of beauty. This was one instance when I gathered up enough courage to call a few key people in Congress to urge passage of this bill!

The highway program in this nation is staggering in its size. During our years in the White House, it was thirty-five times as large as the Panama Canal, Grand Coulee Dam, and the Saint Lawrence Seaway combined—an enormous amount of public property, open to all and for the service of all. We are the road-buildingest nation on earth. And inevitably highways affect the lives of the people, for better or for worse. Therein lies both the glory and the burden of road building. In disturbing so much of the turf of this beautiful country, we incur a special debt not only in terms of land use but also in an aesthetic sense. We are obligated to leave the country looking as good if not better than we found it.

As the country grows, more roads, more parking facilities, more bridges,

Buttercup *(Ranunculus* sp.*)*, Oregon.
STEVE TERRILL

more cuts and fills are required. We are a nation on wheels, and our affluence and leisure have whetted our appetite to enjoy the journey, not just to head for the destination.

Most of the news stories about the highway legislation featured the fact that it provided funds and authority to screen automobile junkyards and control billboards along the nation's major highways. That was a dramatic and evident need, but a less publicized and more exciting facet of the act, to my mind, was that Congress appropriated three additional cents for each dollar spent to be used for the acquisition and maintenance of beauty spots adjacent to the highways.

States could use their money for such items as a scenic overlook, an untouched stand of timber where travelers can picnic, or marking the entrance to each state by planting some of the trees and flowers most typical of it. For instance, glossy magnolia and crepe-myrtle in the deep South; giant saguaro cactus rising like sentinels in Arizona and the West, fields of purple lupine in Wyoming, tall evergreens in the great Northwest—all these offer wonderful possibilities and speak of the state's individuality. I love the sense of regional identity I feel when I cross the state line into Florida and am met by palmettos and palms.

The public tends to take safety and utility for granted when driving the highways. What people remember most are masses of blooming flowers, stunning vistas, and delightful camping and picnic spots. As one highway official put it, "That's what brings in the fan mail."

Tongue in cheek, someone once wrote that I had done what every politician wishes he could do: I had associated myself with an issue as close to home as inflation, as popular as a tax cut, and as necessary as national security.

Well, I've never been a politician, and in this instance the issue claimed me! *Awareness of the environment marched across the stage of our White House years, but results came not from any decree but from the national will. A whole army of people deserves the credit: those indefatigable members of our committee, legislators from the local level on up to Congress, city officials and planners, architects, road builders, developers and landscapers—the wide spectrum of those whose work and decisions affect the looks of our world; but most especially, everyday citizens with eyes to see and the determination to improve what they saw. I count it as one of the great privileges of my life to have served and worked alongside them.*

Avalanche lily *(Erythronium montanum)*, Washington. GLENN VAN NIMWEGEN

Return to Eden: New Landscapes for America

The concepts of Eden and paradise are linked to the need for a spiritual oasis; verdant, fragrant, beautiful, and sheltered, it is a place to refresh the soul, a place of *re*creation in the sense of the original meaning of the word. Since the beginning of time man has built gardens in order to satisfy this need. Although it has something to do with mental well-being, in a garden we are reminded, too, that we are biological creatures, more related to living plants than to the world of steel, masonry, and technology in which we find ourselves every day. So insensitive have we grown to the ersatz that often we find it difficult to separate the fake from the real; we bulldoze fields of real daisies to make parking lots and plant plastic daisies where real ones once grew.

While the basic function of gardens as oases has remained the same through time, the expression of that concept changes to meet new needs in new times. The earliest gardens were rigidly enclosed; even today, the idea of enclosure is considered part of the garden concept. Enclosure served to shut out cold and hot winds, noise, uninvited people, the blazing sun. Within these protected spaces were created idealized worlds, expressed in terms of the time: the geometry and everywhere-flowing water of Persian gardens or the exquisitely rendered mountainscapes of China. Illustrations of Eden as expressed by artists through time reveal their own views of what the ideal was; there are Classical Rome Edens, Italian Renaissance Edens, Moorish Edens, Elizabethan Edens, Capability Brown English Landscape Edens, and, of course, many Elizabeth Barrett Browning Victorian Edens dripping with tearful willows, mournful Norway spruces, ferns, and, wherever possible, sprigs of bleeding-heart and forget-me-not. When we look at gardens of the past we must accept them as expressions of the time in which they were made, and of the needs of the people who made them and how they envisioned an idealized world.

Great parks of the past—Versailles, Windsor, Schönbrunn—were created as

Iris (*Iris tenax*), Oregon. PAT O'HARA

Mexican gold poppy (*Eschscholtzia mexicana*) and owl's clover (*Orthocarpus purpuracens*), Arizona.

private preserves of royal houses; others belonged to the nobility and aristocracy. While some of these were open to the public, it was not until the mid-nineteenth century that public parks as such came into being. Frederick Law Olmsted came back home to America from England as a missionary after seeing the park at Birkenhead in 1852 that had been created for public use. In 1853 the site for New York's Central Park was selected. This, of course, was the pacesetter for the great municipal parks of America. Later, in 1872, Yellowstone National Park was established and the National Park movement got under way. Although not gardenlike in the usual physical sense, these parks serve as oases to refresh the spirit and in that sense are gardens redefined to meet needs of a different time.

The Move Toward the "Natural"

The need for relief from the artificiality of our surroundings has been strikingly demonstrated within the past ten or fifteen years by the demand of Americans for "natural" products and techniques: natural fibers, natural foods, solar energy, earth-sheltered houses, wood stoves, and handmade furniture, quilts, wooden-ware, and pottery. Whole neighborhoods are being restored to wipe away the fake and get back to the real thing.

Tied in with this desire to return to the natural is a reaction to the homogenization of America. The so-called International School of architecture brought about so much sameness in cities that it is difficult to tell one place from another. So strong is the desire to maintain individuality that organized groups in cities, towns, and villages are now fighting to retain the qualities that distinguish where they live from other places.

The same attitudes are extending to countryside landscapes. Native trees, shrubs, wildflowers, and grasses are being seen in a new light, not only as roadside beautifiers and water and labor conservers but as another expression of "the real thing." There is a new desire to allow (or help) Ohio look like Ohio, Oregon like Oregon, New Hampshire like New Hampshire, North Carolina like North Carolina, and Texas like Texas. Even for the passing interstate motorists, the long gardens of our highways can help develop not only keener awareness of the distinctive features of each passing landscape but new consciousness of the variation and richness of the American landscape as a whole—that, indeed, each place is "different." Because each species occurs only in certain habitats, wildflowers and native plants help identify the differences.

The Wildflower Movement

Present-day interest in wildflowers as an organized movement dates from a plea for the protection of native plants and vegetation made by the director of the Missouri Botanic Garden, William Trelease, at a meeting of the American Association for the Advancement of Science, in 1900. The following year, a group of botanists at Harvard University underwrote the formation of the Society for the Protection of Native Plants, with Mrs. Asa Gray, the wife of the eminent botanist, as honorary president. In 1901 Olivia and Caroline Phelps Stokes initiated

Plantain (*Plantago lanceolata*) CARLTON B. LEES

Hibiscus (*Hibiscus palustris, H. Moscheutos* sub sp. *palustris*) CARLTON B. LEES the founding of a national society with a grant of $3,000 to the New York Botanical Garden for the investigation and preservation of native plants. Elizabeth Britton, a recognized bryologist, with her husband, Nathaniel Lord Britton, then director of the Garden, founded the Wildflower Preservation Society of America in 1902. By 1918 Mrs. Britton had to turn to the Smithsonian Institution for help. In Boston the New England Conservation Committee of the Garden Club of America was established, which, in turn, evolved into today's New England Wildflower Society. There are now in existence several active regional, state, and local wildflower societies. The National Wildflower Research Center was founded in 1982 to serve as a clearinghouse for research and educational programs for these many organizations and to assist in the distribution of information, particularly the use of wildflowers in landscape management.

Daylily seedlings (*Hemerocallis* sp.)
CARLTON B. LEES

Aster (*Aster* sp.)
CARLTON B. LEES

But even before the organized movement came about, wildflower interest was high, as revealed by the 1894 publication *Wild Flowers of America* by The Botanical Fine Art Weekly. Testimonials to the quality, desirability, and usefulness of the publication were given by eighteen congressmen, in addition to J. Sterling Morton, President Cleveland's secretary of agriculture. The introductory pages state: "These portfolios are being issued in connection with several prominent newspapers for the sake of placing them within the reach of the multitude, and during the limited time that certain newspapers have the privilege of securing them to their readers at a special figure, the price is 15 cents. A charge beyond this should be reported to the publishers."

In the East, with its essentially woodsy natural landscape, wildflower gardening tended to focus on woodland plants. So many of the plants of open spaces were of foreign origin that they were dismissed as weeds. They also lacked the refinement and appeal of woodland plants, a higher percentage of which were native.

Except to the truly sophisticated, deserts were seen as strange, foreign, and without beauty. Easterners carried their front lawn concepts with them to Phoenix, Reno, Albuquerque, and southern California, where they were totally out of place in an ecological sense. They consumed great amounts of water in lands with limited water supplies in order to carry out an inappropriate fashion in a new place and time. Had the transplanted easterners looked at their surrounding landscapes with unprejudiced eyes, they might have discovered an unfamiliar beauty they could have learned to live with rather than in contradiction to.

In the coastal regions and mountain slopes of Washington, Oregon, and California, interest was stimulated by the fact that so many of the indigenous plants are unique to the area and unlike those found elsewhere. The much-varied ecological situations—some very restricted—gave rise to a large and richly diversified flora. Some of the choicest plants in world horticulture originated here.

While the kind of popular interest in wildflowers and native landscapes typical of eastern portions of the country seems to have arisen later in the prairie states, it is from these states that new leadership has come. Its concerns, rather than those of the botanist–horticulturist, have more to do with landscapes as systems. The inroads of agriculture and its tagalong foreign plants had so changed midland America that few pre-agriculture examples of prairies remained. The focus, then, was on restoration and preservation rather than on numbers of species or aesthetics alone. From this approach came serious research that led to an understanding of prairie ecology and large-scale use and management of native plants. Native grasses and wildflowers came to be understood not only for their aesthetic contribution to the landscape but as elements or components essential to ecologically responsible landscape management. European and East Coast tradition and prejudice had obstructed our vision of the prairie; what seemed monotony became, with observation and understanding, rich and beautiful diversity.

Roadside and Highway Planting

The concept of landscaped roadsides is by no means a recent one in the United States. The parkways of large cities were created as pleasant, recreational "drives" into the suburbs and country but are more related to the tradition of urban parks than to natural countryside. Local highway plantings often were the result of efforts by nonprofessionals and were apt to be *jardinesque* in approach. Using introduced trees and shrubs available in local nurseries, they had little to do with recognition of natural landscapes, native plants, or wildflowers. It was a decorative rather than ecological approach.

A major emphasis for large-scale preservation of rural landscapes and native plant species came from the Midwest in the person of Jens Jensen. While the Olmsted tradition was still dominant in the shaping of municipal and regional parks and cemeteries (and it was, after all, English Landscape School in origin), Jens Jensen looked at midwestern America and saw it for itself. He became a pioneeer. As the "prairie" landscape architect, he stimulated new awareness of and appreciation for these grassland landscapes and the plants inhabiting them. As president of the Friends of Our Native Landscape, in Illinois, Jensen let his insight shine through in a report from the Committee on Roadside Planting and Development (1932):

> There is a rural community in southern Wisconsin that is successfully working out a plan of highway beautification made possible by the voluntary giving of easements consisting of a narrow strip of land paralleling the highway fence lines. . . . Old fences . . . are set back to the new line . . . and planting may then be done within the bounds of the widened highway. . . . The easement still belongs to its original owner, but the authorities of the town assume charge of the native growth found growing on it or may make new planting. . . . It might be possible to acquire additional planting width along many Illinois highways in a similar manner, thereby helping to preserve for posterity our fast disappearing wild flowers. Lands thus given are at present in line with the policy of crop reductions and could easily be encouraged by making such lands tax free.

Highways are no longer what they were when this report was authorized in 1932, but Jensen's concepts cannot be invalidated. Unfortunately, it was not his kind of thinking that dominated road building, else we would not today be exposed to so much of the ugliness that assails us. Commercial development and landscape considerations do not have to be antagonistic, but there seems to be a public-be-damned, gross lack (or not even an inkling) of sensitivity abroad in much of the land. Peter Blake, in his book *God's Own Junkyard,* 1964, calls it "slurb."

Fortunately, slurbs are not everywhere. Get away from the Boston-to-Washington, Atlanta, Chicago, Los Angeles, and other dense population sprawls, and country—real country—can be found again. Mountain, valley, and farmland vistas unobstructed by billboards exist in Vermont; great sweeps of prairie in Nebraska; Arizona desert in which massive, thorny cacti arise from springtime carpets of sparkling, fragile annuals; sky-reaching forests in northern California; and the gentle land forms of the Hill Country of Texas covered at first with bluebonnet, then with Indian paintbrush, delicate pink phlox, crimson blanket flower, pink evening primrose, and golden coreopsis.

Sweet-rocket
or Matrimony
(Hesperis matronalis)
CARLTON B. LEES

Several states have undertaken vigorous programs to plant roadsides with native wildflowers. In eastern states there is more dependence on native perennials and introduced annuals and biennials. Because in its original state the region was forest, it has relatively few plants indigenous to open areas. In the Midwest, many of the European plants that were introduced along with agriculture constitute a very high percentage of what are considered wildflowers. In the drier regions of the southern Great Plains, a smaller percentage of the wildflowers are of foreign origin because climatic conditions are less hospitable to plants from areas having more rainfall and richer soils. Also, in these dry, very hot summer areas a larger percentage of the wildflowers are annual rather than perennial. Within the short span of four or five months these plants can grow to maturity and produce seed before summer heat and drought occur. The seed of these annuals may remain dormant in the soil for several years if necessary (as in the desert) until conditions are again favorable to germination and growth.

Texas initiated its roadside planting program in 1929, when mowing was first curtailed until after existing plants had produced seed. In 1932 the Highway Department hired a landscape architect and perfected the technique of mulch planting; the "hay" from wildflowers was distributed to sections of highway where none grew. Seed dislodged from the hay during the mowing and gathering process ensures that enough remains on the first site, but the hay also carries enough seed to supply the new site. Through continuation of this easy and inexpensive technique, over 77,000 miles of state-maintained highway (1,050,000 acres) are now blanketed with wildflowers at an annual savings of $8 million compared to the regular mowing programs more common to highway maintenance.

Because of increased labor costs, new awareness of the potential contamination of soil and streams by fertilizers and herbicides, and dwindling water supplies, many states are conducting research and testing new techniques of roadside management. Nebraska has made great strides not only in roadside management per se but in preservation and restoration of prairies and in public education about them. Massachusetts has tested wildflower sods that lead to quick

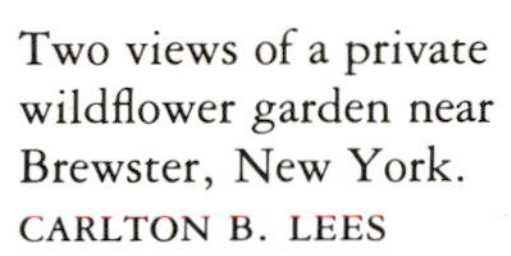

Two views of a private wildflower garden near Brewster, New York.
CARLTON B. LEES

results and avoid erosion problems associated with seeding steep banks and hilly landscapes. Indiana, Virginia, North Carolina, Illinois, Wisconsin, California, Iowa, Oklahoma, and other states are giving serious study to the topic. It is ironic that it is reduced budgets that have stimulated the adoption of techniques that have been obvious for a very long time: it is more economical to work with nature than against it.

Unfortunately, there is much lack of understanding of this concept. Too many state highway departments are caught between the political forces who want to join the popular (and newsworthy) trend to "beautify" their respective states and the uninformed constituents who want "those damned weeds mowed down." It is difficult for people to understand the ecological point of view. We live in a society that demands instant gratification with minimum effort; that is why plastic daisies are popular. The responsible approach requires time and the slow evolution of techniques and results. On the other hand, it is courting disaster to remove all existing desirable plants—no matter how common—in an effort to achieve the California-hillside-covered-with-poppies look, or to try to make some other place look like Texas Hill Country; this leads to destruction of plants, native or not, that already may be performing as part of an ecological niche. In effect, some so-called wildflower plantings are no more than beds of annual flowers and grasses; maintenance is costly and damage to the landscape immeasurable. Roadside and other wildflower plantings require knowledge and respect for the existing landscape; they are not to be undertaken lightly.

Corporate Wildflower Landscapes

The movement of corporations to suburbia and rural areas has given rise to a new kind of landscape, the corporate park. Some of these are the province of a single, large corporation; some are the result of the coming together of two or more separate corporations in a unified parklike setting.

Some of the same factors that stimulated the use of native plants and wildflowers in roadside management—ecological responsibility, respect for surrounding countryside, reduced maintenance costs—have come under consideration here, too. Most corporations are very sensitive to public reaction; they often risk criticism in the early stages of such plantings. But it is also an unusual opportunity to focus on long-term preservation and conservation, issues with which few serious people can take exception. While it is necessary to mollify those suffering from the weedless-golf-green-front-lawn syndrome, the corporation can educate the public, especially by making natural areas and materials available to local schools. It also is necessary that such landscaping not be done hastily or without the services of a well-informed landscape architect, horticulturist, ecologist, and other professionals. How the public perceives the landscape is of utmost importance; good design can help people understand the difference between such a landscape and a lot full of weeds.

Wildflowers in the Home Landscape

Wildflower landscapes are not appropriate as part of all home landscapes. They are appropriate in a surprising number of places, however, if they are designed to fit into the surrounding landscape. While a front-lawn-cum-wildflower-meadow may not be appropriate in a suburban subdivision, something of such a meadow can be achieved if designed to be a part of the larger scheme. With a carefully conceived and executed plan in which the wildflowers are given definite place in an overall scheme that also includes consideration of surrounding properties, compromises are made not just in the design sense of relating to existing landscape but with what may be misunderstanding and unsympathetic neighbors as well. In reality all design is compromise: that of making what is to be fit into what is.

To understand a wildflower meadow it is necessary to know something of succession, the process by which a piece of land that has been disturbed in some way through agricultural, lumbering, residential, or other use (so that it is not at its natural, most stable state) returns to that state. For most of the eastern United States, for example, the landscape was forest. Very little was open. Left alone, eastern landscapes for the most part will return to forest. In the process, inconspicuous weeds are followed by wildflowers and grasses, which in turn are followed by shrubs and small trees such as brambles, shrub-dogwoods, junipers, birches. Poplars, willows, swamp maples, and other softwood trees follow until, in the final state, a hardwood forest of oaks, hickories, beeches, and sugar maples arises. Each plant in each step contributes to the next; each is able to arise and grow to supersede existing plants.

The final stage in this process is referred to as climax, the plant cover as climax vegetation. While there are climax eastern deciduous forests, the climax differs in other parts of the country: there are climax grasslands, boreal (coniferous) forests, eastern coastal plains, and even a bit of tropical West Indian in southern Florida.

An eastern front lawn or a flowerbed or a vegetable plot, left alone, would eventually return to climax forest. In other regions they would return to the climax state of that region. So a lawn, in effect, is succession "on hold" due to the way in which it is managed. If a meadow is mostly annuals and some disturbance of the soil occurs each year, it is closer to agriculture; if it contains perennial wildflowers and grasses and the division is made at the point where shrubs and trees are prevented from growing, then the meadow is yet another step or two up the ladder toward climax landscape. The dynamics of succession are ever-present and fundamental. Understanding this basic concept is necessary to intelligent management of any "natural" landscape, be it preserved, restored, or re-created.

The first step in creating a wildflower meadow at home is to take inventory of plants already existing in the area. Are they growing on constantly disturbed or newly disturbed sites, in pastures subject to grazing, wetlands, roadside ditches, shade? What plants grow together? Since ecological responsibility calls for minimum use or elimination of fertilizers, pesticides, herbicides, and irrigation, it is logical to take the first clues from plants that maintain themselves in landscapes free of such management. It also is necessary to establish goals. Is the goal a meadow exclusively of native plants (impossible in the climax-forest

Northeast, where no meadows existed in the natural state), or are introductions that are considered wildflowers acceptable? Is a meadowlike landscape that might include horticultural hybrids of asters, rudbeckias, daisies, daylilies, and beebalm, along with native and introduced wildflowers and grasses, what is wanted? Personal desires, prejudices, and interest take hold. While there are those who would be shocked with the introduction of horticultural plants into a meadow, others are not. A garden should express the people who live in it; therefore, all approaches are valid if the meadow is, in the main, self-sustaining. The meaning of the word *meadow* originates in the concept of grassland that can be mowed—usually for hay. As long as grasses are included, cultivation in the sense of a perennial border or vegetable plot is eliminated, and the basic management technique is that of mowing (usually in the late fall or midwinter), such landscape treatment qualifies as a meadow.

Joe-pye-weed
(*Eupatorium* sp.)
CARLTON B. LEES

Seedling daylily
(*Hemerocallis* sp.),
orange butterfly-weed
(*Asclepias tuberosa*), and
dark red bee-balm
(*Monarda didyma*)
CARLTON B. LEES

Seed Sources and Mixtures

The "wildflower meadow in a can" idea suddenly zoomed into prominence almost as soon as the idea of including wildflowers in managed landscapes came into being. Sealing seed in cans is a good idea, provided the cans are stored at cool temperatures. At the very least, seeds in a can are protected from undesirable humidity. But the weakness of the approach is in the fact that too many irresponsible retailers jumped onto the bandwagon and encouraged the idea that all the purchaser had to do was to go home and scatter the seed just anywhere. Without responsible cultural instructions or information on the effect of regional variations or what would happen the second year and thereafter (even if some success should be attained the first year), but with visions of glorious abundance, carefree childhood in the countryside, or of first love, thousands of these cans were sold to many soon-to-be-disappointed people. With the cans in boutiques and gift catalogs, and advertised in sophisticated magazines, who could resist? It must be recognized, also, that much of the failure resulted from the public naiveté that abounds about the dynamics of the natural world. Happily, a more responsible approach is being taken by at least one producer; he is "canning" individual species of wildflowers and mixtures that are specific for specific situations.

Success with any wildflower planting can be more readily achieved by taking inventory of the kinds growing in similar nearby areas and using this list as a guide in ordering specific species from seed producers and suppliers. If you can get permission to gather seed on property you do not own, mark the plants while in bloom with brightly colored plastic ribbon, then check the plants frequently as seed-ripening time arrives. If you are too early, seed will be green and not ready; if too late, the birds may have devoured it. Large grocery bags make ideal collecting containers; be sure to identify each species on the side of each bag. Excellent instructions for harvesting, cleaning, and storing wildflower seed are given in *Growing and Propagating Wildflowers* by Harry R. Phillips et al. in collaboration with the staff of the North Carolina Botanical Garden, Chapel Hill. This book is basic to wildflower gardening; gathering your own seed guarantees freshness, expands one's perceptions, and is cheap.

Many reliable sources of wildflower seeds and plants are listed in the appendix.

Establishing a Meadow

Methods for starting a wildflower meadow are as varied as are the sites. One approach is to allow a mowed or cultivated plot to remain unmown or uncultivated for one or more growing seasons and observe what happens. In the plot that had been cultivated, in particular, will be an invasion of what Armistead Browning at the University of Delaware calls "supertramps": pigweed, crabgrass, ragweed, chickweed. These are escapes from the earliest seed mixtures that came from Europe and have been persistent in occupying our landscapes ever since. The formerly mowed plot will probably be invaded with dandelion, plantain, and other plants from the same source, and seemingly to the exclusion of others. But remember succession; these plants are but playing a role in the transformation of these sites from one stage to another. Patience, rather than anxiety, is needed. Often the most difficult impatience to deal with is not one's own but that of onlookers. And even upon explanation, the majority will be nonbelievers. In the second year more acceptable plants will appear, shading out the supertramps and other unwanted species. At this point hand-removal of any new undesirables and the introduction of seedlings of wanted species will speed up the process.

Another approach calls for destroying all existing vegetation with one of the herbicides that rapidly degrade and do not leave contaminating residues in the soil. About two weeks later, till the soil and repeat herbicide treatment when residual weeds reappear. Then, after another three or four weeks, lightly rake the tilled soil and sow wildflower seed. The seed, lightly covered, can be mulched with straw, dry and seedless grass clippings, wildflower "hay" (such as described in the Texas Highway Department technique), or even vermiculite. In all cases, however, the mulch should be applied in a thin layer; its function is to conserve soil moisture and protect seedlings from dehydrating wind and complete exposure to sun —visualize it as a protective net. Under no conditions use agricultural hay as a mulch; it contains too many seeds of plants eradicated with the herbicide treatment and would only reintroduce them. The meadow must be watered thoroughly. Use a lawn sprinkler and make sure the soil is moist to a depth of about two inches before turning it off or moving it to another portion of the newly seeded meadow. Be sure to keep the soil continuously moist through the early weeks of fragile seedling growth. With this treatment, residual weeds will be at a minimum; the wildflower seedlings will predominate. Seed of desirable grasses also should be included in the seed mixture. Those that grow in clumps are best because they leave interstices for flowering plants. Grasses that form mats (desirable in lawn grasses) are detrimental in a wildflower meadow because they create a solid cover and prevent seed from reaching soil where it can germinate and ensure the continuation of the meadow. These "ideal" lawn grasses also are highly

Bee-balm (*Monarda didyma*) and orchard grass (*Dactylis glomerata*)
CARLTON B. LEES

competitive for water and soil nutrients.

Depending on where it is and what the invasive species tend to be, the use of herbicide may be necessary for establishing or maintaining a wildflower meadow. While brambles can be kept in check by annual mowing, they send out more branches each year. The plants can be removed by hand-digging, but in many places they are so numerous that the task is overwhelming. The use of herbicide as "spot treatment" (on an individual plant-by-plant basis) can eliminate such plants. If done with great care, particularly by physical application with a brush, sponge, or wet glove (over a rubber glove) rather than by spraying, damage to surrounding plants is nil. The newer herbicides soon break down into naturally occurring minerals, so no harmful residues remain in the soil, even if spilled.

Other Wildflower Landscapes

Establishing a wildflower meadow, prairie landscape, wetland planting, or restoring a desert or alpine landscape is no small job. It requires patience, time, attention, devotion, knowledge, and hard work. Once established, however, the rewards are endless. Such landscapes change from day to day, week to week, season to season, and no two years are alike. The manner in which plants grow together, what dominates or succumbs to what: these are dynamics to be observed. While in the eastern forestland certain techniques are appropriate, other techniques are applicable to other places (the hay-mulch seeding technique of the Texas roadside has been described), but the ecological conditions vary so much from one portion of the country to another that it is impossible to describe all techniques here. The point is that it is necessary to understand something of the fundamental natural processes involved, to inventory conditions and plants of the area under consideration, observe what already is going on, and then seek specific information from local sources. Sometimes it is not always easy to find those sources because they extend from governmental agencies to local universities, county conservation commissions, local chapters of national environmental organizations, garden clubs, and other groups. National organizations and institutions such as the National Wildflower Research Center are prepared to provide names of local sources of specific regional information.

A wildflower landscape, no matter where it may be, has the potential to contribute more to one's understanding of natural forces than almost any other experience. The fact that such experience is available on a day-by-day basis when a wildflower meadow or other piece of natural landscape is incorporated into the home landscape adds enormously to its impact. This is particularly true for small children who can then develop an early awareness of the interrelationships of plants, insects, birds, and small mammals. Profound lessons learned early in life are apt to be lasting. And not the least of the lessons to learn is that one can create beauty through one's own effort. "It is the desire to achieve an end," wrote Derek Clifford in *A History of Garden Design,* 1966, "which makes a work of art valid, not the desire to display ingenuity in the employment of the means."

National Wildflower Research Center

Common sunflower (*Helianthus annuus*), Colorado.
RANDY TRINE/DRK

Recording data on the germination of Indian blanket in marked plots. JOSE AZEL

As I look back across a span of more than seven decades, I'm grateful for the joy that nature has given me and for the lifetime of experiences that led me to believe I might repay a part of the debt I've incurred for beauty enjoyed.

In 1982, at age seventy, I decided it was now or never! The children were grown and, so to speak, the "crop's in the barn"—the LBJ Library and School of Public Affairs on which Lyndon and I had worked so long were successful and stable, and our family business was well managed and moving along. I felt a certain freedom to "do my own thing." My efforts to grow wildflowers had resulted in some successes and at least as many failures. The question marks that grew in my mind seemed to me my largest crop by far! I wanted to have a hand in finding the answers. *The years had passed, work had claimed more of my life and adventure less, but now I found myself once more daring to venture into the unexplored.*

The National Wildflower Research Center was launched on December 22, 1982, with a gift of sixty acres of land our family owned just east of Austin on farm-to-market Road 973 and "seed money" of $125,000—my birthday present to the people of this land I've traveled so much and love so dearly. The only structure on the land was a small house, which was soon to be converted into an office/laboratory. I remember that windy December day so vividly—a happy crowd of friends who had joined the Center's one-hundred-member board of trustees, plenty of folks from the press who would get the word out about the Center, and a throng of onlookers cheering us on.

We arrived at the site (normally somewhat forlorn at this time of year) on gaily decorated buses. A tent had been set up with displays of wildflower photographs all around and plenty of cake and coffee. There were two huge Oriental rugs on the ground (arranged for by my ingenious friend and trustee Patsy Steves) and bales of hay scattered here and there. The centerpiece of this rather incongruous arrangement was a grand piano! A band played, brief speeches were made, entertainment followed, and then we prepared to get under way! I recall how especially proud I'd been to announce that committee-member Laurance Rockefeller made a gift of $125,000 to match my own, my fellow directors from Texas Commerce Bank in Houston donated $25,000, and there was a host of checks from lifetime friends for $25, $40, $50, $100.

With this beginning, our nonprofit organization set about working toward our purpose: for the Center to become a catalyst to stimulate the preservation, propagation, and increased use of wildflowers and native plants throughout the United States.

Some may wonder how I chose wildflowers when there are hunger and unemployment and the big bomb in the world. Well, I, for one, think we will *survive, and I hope that along the way we can keep alive our experience with the flowering earth—for the bounty of nature is also one of the deep needs of man.*

The world in which many wildflowers grew and flourished, their native habitat, is disappearing, necessarily so because the population has doubled in the past fifty years. Meadows and fields and wild places I knew as a young woman have been filled with grids of housing developments, shopping malls, industrial parks, and ribbons of highways. A century ago, William Cullen Bryant looked with his poet's eyes at America's "unshorn fields, boundless and beautiful," and with his poet's voice said: "I think I hear the sound of that advancing multitude which shall soon fill these fields."

And the multitudes have come! *We can, however, plan to keep some of nature's bounty in suitable places, if we have the knowledge and foresight. Public areas are natural locations for planting wildflowers and native plants. The rights-of-way along the roadsides, public parks and parklands, historic restorations, campuses and school grounds are excellent candidates for wildflower plantings, as are private lands such as residential developments, corporate parks, churchyards, and our own homes—in appropriate areas, of course. We're not advocating doing away with pleasurable green lawns and shrubs! But there are many instances when they can be mixed with nature.*

(Top and bottom) Lady Bird Johnson dedicating the National Wildflower Research Center near Austin, Texas, on December 22, 1982. Nash Castro, founding president of the Center, stands with her in the bottom photograph.
FRANK WOLFE

Today in an era when water tables are dropping and the costs of maintaining public landscapes like city parks are soaring, we need the gallant persistence of these plants that demand less attention than thirsty hybrid grasses and garden exotics. Texas alone is yearly pumping 5.7 million acre-feet more water out of our aquifers than nature refills. Wildflower landscapes can help us save water. Wildflowers also can save time and maintenance money. They may even bring money to cities and states. Wildflower trails and flower festivals improve local pride and bring in tourists. But, as I've said, we need to know much more about how and when and where to plant them to get reliable, predictable, consistent results. We need that knowledge if we are to preserve wildflowers and to choose them as complements to traditional manicured landscaping.

In planting conventional flowers or vegetable gardens, we have a wealth of helpful catalogs and publications to tell us which plants are suited to a particular soil, or sun or shade or wind and weather conditions. We know how long garden seeds need to germinate and whether they should be planted deep or shallow. In farming we have the benefit of centuries of observation—close observation because our ancestors' very lives depended on knowing just what and when and how to plant. We have the benefit of a Department of Agriculture and the research carried on by state schools of agriculture and horticulture. But because wildflowers have not been thought essential to life and to the economy, little research has been done on them. Slowly we are beginning to realize that there are hard, practical, economic reasons for using wildflowers in our landscapes, and reasons of the soul as well—for our peace of mind, our emotions and spirit are conditioned by what our eyes see.

Wildflowers are photographed in all stages of growth for the seedling identification project. JOSE AZEL

Civic-minded men and women see the economic potential. A major developer in Dallas gave $25,000 to the city's parks department to purchase seed for highway median strips in that city. Another in Houston is using native plants as the basic planting around an extensive housing project. And there are so many more examples.

Grand Teton Lodge Company in Wyoming is a project we're watching with great interest. It committed $60,000 for wildflower landscaping at its Jackson Hole Golf and Tennis Club for the golf-course perimeter and rough areas.

In New Jersey and New York, the Palisades Interstate Parkway has a new wildflower project, partly inspired by our Texas Highway Department and very much by Nash Castro, our Center's president.

And there are many more stories to tell!

But back to the Center. From our modest beginnings, we set about hiring a director, Dr. David Northington, and a vigorous, small staff willing to tackle any job that comes along. We've also been joined by an energetic band of volunteers, including college students and members of Austin's Junior League. A national membership program was mapped out with a grant from the Lila Acheson Wallace Foundation, and at present (December 1986) we claim over 8,000 members. We now have a new building with a small laboratory, and two small greenhouses. Our computerized clearinghouse operation is running in high gear, finding out who is doing what in this field all over the country, so we can provide that information to all who care—facts from laboratory research and dirt-gardening experiences that will make a big difference in community beauty and budgets. My *heart lies in the two-hundred-plus test plots and twenty acres of demonstration areas we have put in, using different kinds of seed and varying planting methods and research treatments. From them, we will learn what works best, solving some of nature's puzzles in our area, and providing clues for plant lovers elsewhere.*

As I write this on the Wildflower Center's fourth anniversary, I'd like to share some of the Center's achievements:

—Research efforts now include cooperative ventures with universities, botanical gardens, and arboreta—in New York (three different areas), Georgia (two sites), South Carolina (three sites), South Dakota, Colorado, Arizona, and Texas (six sites). An additional three sites are being planned.

—Three years of field-plot data on commercially available wildflower-seed mixes tell us that the locally native and long-naturalized species work the best in the Southwest.

—Our national planting trials have helped us establish how best to select a site, prepare the ground, seed, and manage wildflower plantings, and when to do a planting. This information is printed up for members and the general public who write to the Center.

—A list of commercially available wildflowers, native grasses, shrubs, and trees has been developed that can be used in a landscape to provide almost year-round color (colorscaping) for some parts of the country. This is being constantly updated.

—Our research on bluebonnet establishment has demonstrated that the use of

Research botanists carefully study wildflowers and prepare specimens for the Center's herbarium.
JOSE AZEL

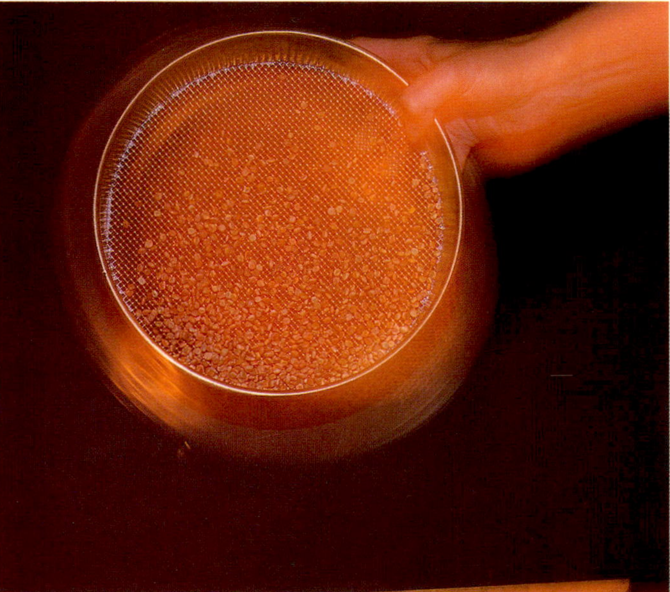

(Top left and bottom right) Education of the young and greater public awareness of wildflowers are major priorities for the Center, which sponsors school tours of the facilities. JOSE AZEL. (Top right) Executive Director David Northington often addresses outside groups on the subject of wildflowers. Here he stands with the projected image of a pink evening primrose. JOSE AZEL. (Bottom left) Wildflower seeds are separated through sieves of varying meshes from all extraneous matter before being used in research plantings. JOSE AZEL

a rhizobium *inoculant improves establishment and flowering. This coating on the seeds stimulates bacteria in the soil necessary for the growth of seedlings.*

—We have obtained practical knowledge about the use of modified grain drills (drill seeders), flail mowers, soil pulverizers, disk harrows, and other equipment used to plant large-scale wildflower projects successfully.

Education is another goal, and we can count the following among our accomplishments:

—Our quarterly newsletter, Wildflower, *has received acclaim for the informative "how to" articles as well as the news of national events and other helpful information that we include.*

—Six national symposia, in New York, Washington, D.C., and Georgia, as well as in the Southwest, have been cosponsored by the Center. We have participated in an additional sixteen seminars and national meetings at universities and arboreta around the country.

—The Center's national information clearinghouse has responded to public inquiries on a wide range of wildflower subjects, and the number of inquiries has grown from 2,000 a year to over 21,000 a year.

—Several Public Broadcasting stations have included information about the Center's work, as have a number of newspapers and magazines.

Generally, our findings indicate the importance of the following information:

—Use wildflowers that are indigenous to your area, or, if using a commercial mix, select the one with fewest nonindigenous species in it.

—Don't exceed the recommended seeding rate. It's expensive and it doesn't improve the density of the result. (We make an exception for a one-time seeding of bluebonnets.)

—Make sure your seed is in good contact with the soil. Soil-seed contact *is the name of the game! A drill seeder works best for medium to large plantings; an adaptation of an agricultural grain drill, it provides for even distribution of each variety at the recommended seeding rate, and plants larger seed underground. At this time there isn't a drill seeder on the market of a size that would be of practical use to the homeowner. If the demand increases for this product, it will surely appear on the market.*

—Water new plantings, if rains are not timely. Seeds do need water to germinate and become established.

—Fall seeding is recommended, especially in the southern half of the United States for most wildflowers.

—Do not clip or mow, if possible, until all the wildflowers have finished setting seed.

All this is just a beginning, but in time, with more funds and professional and amateur help, the Center hopes to learn a great deal about how to make nature's accidental gardens more dependable.

In his book Pioneering with Wildflowers, *former senator George Aiken of Vermont wrote: "The old frontier days of America are over, but the last stand of some of our wildflowers presents to us a new frontier in which we can adventure." I heartily agree with the senator and am thankful that so many young people (and those young in spirit) see nature—whether as a hiker or a microbiologist or dedicated gardener—as a place in which to adventure and discover.*

Saving our legacy of wildflowers is something I am convinced can be accomplished with the right combination of workable ideas and citizens with spirit. How much poorer our world would be without this bounty! I think of the words of an old Texas Ranger written in 1875: "All of western Texas was a real frontier, and for one who loved nature and God's own creation, it was a paradise on earth. In the springtime one could travel for hundreds of miles on a bed of flowers. Sometimes they came up to my stirrups. O how I wish I had the power to describe the wonderful country as I saw it then!"

For my seven grandchildren and everybody else's, I hope we can keep a part of that vision in our public and private landscapes. In our quest for a better future, I have faith that an appreciation for values of the past, and for the beauty and health of this natural world we all share, will be high on our agenda.

A field of phlox, horse mint, and Gaillardia near the entrance to the LBJ Ranch, Stonewall, Texas. DENNIS FAGAN

Lady Bird Johnson seated among the blossoms of Indian paintbrush, Texas bluebonnet, and Engelmann's daisy. DENNIS FAGAN

Gaillardia in bloom along the banks of the Pedernales River. DENNIS FAGAN

Mrs. Johnson seated in a field of Drummond's phlox, welcoming visitors to the LBJ Ranch. DENNIS FAGAN

Afterword

Gardens, farms, fields, plants, and wildflowers always have been part of my life. Like Mrs. Johnson, I can't remember when they weren't "just there" as an ordinary part of every day. For me, perhaps some of this experience was due to ancestry, but some was due to surroundings. My grandmother's garden was bright with yellow tulips, multi-faced pansies, and all sorts of roses. I remember as a small child, particularly, a heavily clove-scented ornamental current and dark red-purple lilacs in which I could bury my face and inhale delicious sweetness. In the country, on a family farm, we had a small cottage (always called The Shack); here I was surrounded by the wildflowers of woodlands, pastures, and meadows. Violets, buttercups, daisies, giant thistles, lady's-slippers, and marsh marigolds were abundant. In the pasture cows ate around the woolly-leaved rosettes of mullein, which sent tall, yellow-flowered spikes skyward. I remember having to obey the order not to run through the meadows before mowing time; cutting grass for hay requires upward-standing not trampled stalks. The ox-eye daisies and black-eyed Susans always seemed to be at their prime just as mowing began, but I could gather long-stemmed bunches of them at the meadow edges, put them in pails on the porch, and take them to the city on Sunday night.

As I got older and sometimes helped with turning and winnowing hay as it dried, and with loading it onto the horse-drawn wagon and heading for the barn, I felt a certain sadness over the lost daisies and black-eyed Susans but it was partly overcome with the experience of sunshine, blue skies, the sweet scent of freshly mown hay, and the sure knowledge that all would return again next year. The harsher reality of the heat of the barn's mow, of seed and chaff sticking to sweaty arms, back, chest, and penetrating my nostrils, eyes, ears, and mouth had less to do with the beauty of the daisies than with the overwhelming urge to get the job done and be out of there, but I still love meadows with their grasses, daisies, and black-eyed Susans. They have been a part of my life and will be, always.

Yellow lady's-slipper *(Cypripedium calceolus)*, Michigan. JOHN GERLACH/DRK

Ox-eye daisy *(Chrysanthemum leucanthemum)*, Michigan. ROD PLANCK

Wherever I have traveled I have tried to observe and learn from landscapes no matter how unfamiliar they may be or different from those of my native New England. Discovering the Sonoran Desert, the piney woods of the South, the misty coastlands of the Pacific Northwest, and, of course, the Texas Hill Country has been a series of adventures. I have thought and always hoped that if more of us could experience this adventure we would be more aware of our own biological origin, sense our relationship to the natural processes, and perhaps better appreciate the landscape around us. We live in and find ourselves in a constantly more artificial world; we need wildflowers to keep us from becoming artificial, too.

And that also is what wildflowers are about.

Selected Bibliography

Aiken, George. *Pioneering with Wild Flowers.* Vermont: Privately printed, 1935.

Anderson, Edgar. *Plants, Man and Life.* London: Andrew Melrose, 1954.

Ash, David, and Ash, Nancy B. "A Chronology of the Development of Prehistoric Horticulture in Westcentral Illinois." Center for American Archeology, Laboratory Report no. 56, 1982.

Bacon, Francis. "On Gardening." London, 1625.

Bailey, Liberty Hyde, and Zoe, Ethel. *Hortus Third.* Revised and expanded by the staff of the Liberty Hyde Bailey Hortorium. New York: Macmillan Co., 1976.

Bates, Marston. *The Forest and the Sea.* New York: Random House, 1960.

Blake, Peter. *God's Own Junkyard.* New York: Holt, Rinehart and Winston, 1964.

Botanical Fine Arts Weekly. *Wild Flowers of America.* 1894.

Bradbury, John. *Travels in the Interior of America in the Years 1809, 1810, and 1811.* Liverpool, 1817.

Catesby, Mark. *The Natural History of Carolina, Georgia, Florida, and the Bahama Islands.* London, 1731–43.

Clifford, Derek. *A History of Garden Design.* Rev. ed. New York: Praeger, 1966.

Coats, Alice. *Flowers and Their Histories.* New York: Pittman, 1965.

Dana, Charles. *Two Years Before the Mast.* New York: Macmillan Co., 1980.

Darlington, William. *Memorials of John Bartram and Humphry Marshall.* Philadelphia, 1849.

Darwin, Erasmus. *The Botanic Garden. A Poem in Two Parts.* 2d American ed. New York: Columbia College, 1807.

Dodonaeus [Dodoens]. *Historie des Plantes.* 1557; English ed., 1578.

Douglas, David. *Journal of, During His Travels in America, 1823–1827.* London: William Wesley and Son, 1914.

———. *Journal . . . Appendix II.* London: William Wesley and Son, 1914.

Eifert, Virginia S. *Tall Trees and Far Horizons.* New York: Dodd, Mead and Co., 1965.

Fraegri, Knut, and Iverson, Johns. *Textbook of Pollen Analysis.* New York: Hafner, 1964.

Fuchs, Leonhart. *De Historia Stirpium.* Basel, 1542.

Gerard, John. *The Herball or General Historie of Plantes.* London: John Norton, 1597.

Gleason, H. A., and Cronquist, Arthur. *The Natural Geography of Plants.* New York: Columbia University Press, 1964.

Greenwell, Jean. "The Mystery of Kaluakauka." Kona Historical Society. Manuscript, 1986.

Hariot, Thomas. *A Briefe and True Report of the Newfoundland of Virginia . . . drawings Diligently Collected and Drawne by John White.* Frankfurt, 1590.

Index Kewensis. Vols. 1–2 and Supplements. Oxford: Clarendon Press, 1893–95.

Irving, Washington. *Astoria.* Portland, Oregon: Binford Metropolitan, 1836.

James, Edward. *Account of an Expedition from Pittsburgh to the Rocky Mountains, 1819–20.* Philadelphia: American Philosophical Society, 1823.

Jarvis, P. J. "North American Plants and Horticultural Innovation in England, 1550–1700." *Geographical Review* (October 1973).

Johnson, Lyndon B. "Remarks at the University of Michigan." May 22, 1964. Papers of Lyndon B. Johnson.

Kalm, Peter. *Travels in North America.* Journal, 1772.

Kindscher, Kelly. *Edible Wild Plants of the Prairie—An Ethobotanic Guide.* Kansas City: University of Kansas Press, 1987.

Linnaeus. *Species Plantarum.* Stockholm, 1753.

Michaux, André. *Flora Boréali Americana.* Paris, 1803.

Michaux, François André. *North American Silva.* Originally published as *Histoire des arbes forestiers de L'Amérique septentrionale* (Paris, 1810–13).

Missouri Republican (May 7, 1823).

Monardes, Nicholas. *Joyfull Newes out of the Newe Founde Worlde.* Seville, 1569; English ed., 1577.

Nuttall, Thomas. *Genera of North American Plants.* Philadelphia, 1818.

———. "Nuttall's Travels into the Old Northwest, An Unpublished 1810 Diary." Edited by Jeannette Graustein. *Chronica Botanica,* 1951.

Olmsted, Frederick Law. *Walks and Talks of an American Farmer in England.* New York: Putnam and Son, 1852.

Parkinson, John. *Paradisi in Sole Paradisus Terrestris.* London, 1629.

Peterson, Roger Tory, and McKenny, Margaret. *A Field Guide to Wildflowers of Northeastern and North-Central North America.* Boston: Houghton Mifflin Co., 1974.

Phillips, Harry R., et al. *Growing and Propagating Wild Flowers.* Chapel Hill and London: University of North Carolina Press, 1985.

Pursh, Frederick. *Florae Americae Septentrionalis.* London: James Black and Son, 1814.

Stout, A. B. *Daylilies, the Wild Species and Garden Clones of Hemerocallis.* New York: Macmillan Co., 1934.

Stuckey, Ronald L. "Distributional History of *Lythrum salicaria* (Purple Loosestrife) in North America." *Bartonia* 47 (1980).

Teale, Edwin Way. *Journey into Summer.* New York: Dodd, Mead and Co., 1960.

Thwaites, R. G. "Nuttall's Travels into the Arkansa Territory, 1819." *Early Western Travels, 1747–1848.* Cleveland, 1905.

Trelease, William. "Some Twentieth Century Problems." *Science II* 12 (June 3, 1900).

True, Rodney H. "A Sketch of the Life of John Bradbury, Including His Unpublished Correspondence with Thomas Jefferson." *Proceedings of the American Philosophical Society,* Philadelphia (1929).

U.S. Department of Agriculture. *Yearbook, 1941.*

Young, William, Jr. *Botaniste de Pensylvanie.* A list of American plants. Paris: Vilmorin, 1783.

Sources of Regional Wildflower Seed Mixtures

Applewood Seed Co.
5380 Vivian Street
Arvada, CO 80002
(303)431-6283
Will custom mix

Alpine Plants
P.O. Box 245
Tahoe Vista, CA 95732
(916)546-5578
Specialize in Western mountain areas

Botanic Garden Seed Co., Inc.
9 Wyckoff Street
Brooklyn, NY 11202
(718)624-8839

Clyde Robin Seed Co.
25670 Nickel Place
Hayward, CA 94545
(415)785-0425
Will custom mix

Environmental Seed Producers
P.O. Box 5904
El Monte, CA 91734
(818)442-3330
Will custom mix

Great Western Seed Co.
P.O. Box 387
810 Jackson St.
Albany, OR 97321
(503)928-3100
Wholesale only; will custom mix

High Altitude Gardens
P.O. Box 4238
220 Lewis #8
Ketchum, ID 83340
(208)726-3221
Specialize in high-altitude species; will custom mix

Lofts, Inc.
Chimney Rock Road
Bound Brook, NJ 08805
(201)560-1590, 356-8700

McLaughlin's Seeds
P.O. Box 550
Mead, WA 99021
(509)466-0230
Specialize in Pacific Northwest species

Moon Mountain Wildflowers
P.O. Box 34
Morro Bay, CA 93442
(805)772-2473
Will custom mix

Native Plants, Inc.
P.O. Box 177
Leigh, UT 84043
(801)582-0144
Will custom mix

Passiflora Wildflowers
Rt 1, Box 190-A
Germanton, NC 27019
(919)591-5816
Will custom mix

Plants of the Southwest
1812 Second Street
Santa Fe, NM 87501
(505)983-1548
Specialize in Southwestern species; will custom mix

Prairie Moon Nursery
Rt. 3, Box 163
Winona, MN 55987
(507)452-5231, 452-4990
Specialize in prairie mixes; will custom mix

Prairie Nursery
P.O. Box 365
Westfield, WI 53964
(608)296-3679
Specialize in prairie mixes; will custom mix

Prairie Restorations, Inc.
P.O. Box 327
Princeton, MN 55371
(612)389-4342
Specialize in prairie mixes; will custom mix

Prairie Ridge Nursery
RR 2, 9738 Overland Road
Mount Horeb, WI 53572-2832
(608)437-5245
Specialize in prairie mixes; will custom mix

S & S Seeds
P. O. Box 1275
Carpinteria, CA 93013
(805)684-0436
Will custom mix

Stock Seed Farms, Inc.
RR 1, Box 112
Murdock, NE 68407
(402)867-3771
Specialize in prairie mixes; will custom mix

Sun Seeds
P.O. Box 1438
Hollister, CA 95024
(408)636-9505
Wholesale only

Wild Seed
P.O. Box 27751
Tempe, AZ 85282
(602)968-9751
Wholesale only; specialize in Southwestern species

Wildseed, Inc.
16810 Barker Springs
Suite 218
Houston, TX 77084
(713)578-7800
Specialize in Texas species; will custom mix

Wildflowers International, Inc.
918-B Enterprise Way
Napa, CA 94558
(707)253-0570
Wholesale only; will custom mix

Index of Flowers Illustrated

D

E

F

G

Gayfeather *(Liatris punctata),* 140, 184
Gaywing *(Polygala pancifolia),* 161
Gerardia *(G. fasciculata,* now *Agalinis fasciculata),* 85
Ghost orchid *(Polyrrhiza lindenii),* 216
Gigantic Erythronium *(Erythronium giganteum,* now *E. grandiflorum),* 93
Glacier lily *(Erythronium grandiflorum),* 230
Globeflower *(Trollius laxus),* 230
Globe-tulip *(Calochortus albus),* 105
Goldenrod *(Solidago* sp.*),* 35, 50, 185
Grass pink *(Calopogon pulchellus),* 215, 219
Grass widow *(Sisyrinchium douglasii),* 244
Great blue lobelia *(Lobelia siphilitica),* 39, 42, 51

H

Harebell *(Campanula rotundifolia),* 230
Harvest brodiaea *(Brodiaea elegans),* 187
Hawkweed *(Hieracium* sp.*),* 54
Hollow-stemmed Joe-pye-weed *(Eupatorium fistulosum),* 201

I

Indian blanket *(Gaillardia pulchella),* 16, 64, 65, 127, 171
Indian paintbrush *(Castilleja purpurea),* 174
Indian paintbrush *(Castilleja* sp.*),* 25, 31, 125, 131, 146, 175, 223
Indian pipe *(Monotropa uniflora),* 160
Indian pond lily *(Nuphar polysepala),* 197
Iris *(Iris missouriensis),* 200

J

Jack-in-the-pulpit *(Arisaema triphyllum),* 160

K

Knotweed *(Puliginam bistortoides),* 223

L

Lace cactus *(Echinocereus* sp.*),* 176
Lapland rosebay *(Rhododendron lapponicum),* 253
Large-flowered trillium *(Trillium grandiflorum),* 154
Larkspur *(Delphinium* sp.*),* 184
Leafless beaked orchid *(Stenorhynchus orchiodes),* 216
Leopard lily *(Lilium catesbaei),* 164
Leptosiphon *(Linanthus),* 106
Lily-tulip *(Calochortus albus),* 105
Lizard's-tail *(Saururus cernuus),* 201
Lobelia *(Lobelia siphilitica),* 39, 42, 51
Long-spurred violet *(Viola rostrata),* 153
Lupine *(Lupinus nanus),* 105
Lupine *(Lupinus perennis),* 2–3, 78
Lupine *(Lupinus* sp.*),* 25, 78, 122, 125, 146, 170, 174, 175, 240, 241

M

Mariposa tulip *(Calochortus albus),* 105
Marsh blue violet *(Viola cucullata),* 153
Marsh marigold *(Caltha palustris),* 198
Marsh pink *(Sabatia grandiflora),* 77, 84, 167
Mexican hat *(Ratibida columnifera),* 102, 123
Mexican poppy *(Eschscholzia mexicana),* 1
Michigan lily *(Lilium michiganense),* 186
Monkey flower *(Mimulus* sp.*),* 238
Monkshood *(Aconitum columbianum),* 230
Moth mullein *(Verbascum blattaria),* 184
Mountain avens *(Dryas integrifolia),* 253
Mountain heather *(Cassiope tetragona),* 248
Mountain lady's-slipper *(Cypripedium montanum),* 142
Mountain laurel *(Kalmia latifolia),* 10

N

O

P

Q

R

Rabbit brush *(Chrysothamnus nauseosus)*, 243
Ragged fringed orchid *(Habenaria lacera)*, 219
Ragged robin *(Lychnis flos-cuculi)*, 186
Ram's-head lady's-slipper *(Cypripedium arietinum)*, 221
Red clover *(Trifolium pratense)*, 52
Red maple *(Acer rubrum)*, 49
Red phlox *(Phlox drummondii)*, 29, 125, 128, 175
Rock-nettle *(Eucnides bartonioides)*, 172
Rose pogonia *(Pogonia ophioglossoides)*, 219
Rose vervain *(Verbena tampensis)*, 163
Round-lobed hepatica *(Hepatica americana)*, 157
Rue anemone *(Anemonella thalictroides)*, 157

S

Salal *(Gaultheria shallon)*, 244
Sassafras *(Sassafras albidum)*, 51
Scarlet gilia *(Ipomopsis rubra)*, 165
Sea pink *(Sabatia stellaris)*, 77
Seashore mallow *(Kosteletzkya virginica)*, 196
Seaside gentian *(Eustoma exaltatuim)*, 166
Shooting star *(Dodecatheon meadia)*, 80
Shooting star *(Dodecatheon pauciflorum)*, 230
Showy lady's-slipper *(Cypripedium reginae)*, 220
Showy orchid *(Orchis spectabilis)*, 216
Shrubby cinquefoil *(Potentilla fruticosa)*, 190
Skunk cabbage *(Symplocarpus foetidus)*, 194
Small Solomon's seal *(Polygonatum biflorum)*, 158
Sneezeweed *(Hymenoxys* sp.*)*, 231
Snow trillium *(Trillium nivale)*, 154
Spiderwort *(Tradescantia ohiensis)*, 30, 42
Spiderwort *(Tradescantia* sp.*)*, 28, 31
Spiderwort *(Tradescantia virginiana)*, 41
Spotted coralroot *(Corallorhiza maculata)*, 217
Spotted knapweed *(Centauria maculosa)*, 188
Spotted touch-me-not *(Impatiens capensis)*, 158
Spring beauty *(Claytonia virginica)*, 157
Squirrel corn *(Dicentra canadensis)*, 161
Starflower *(Trientalis borealis)*, 157
Star tulip *(Calochortus nudus)*, 231
Sticky geranium *(Geranium viscoissimum)*, 265
Storksbill *(Erodium cicutarium)*, 233
Stream violet *(Viola glabella)*, 153
Striped coralroot *(Corallorhiza striata)*, 217
Sunflower *(Helianthus annuus)*, 45
Swamp lily *(Crinum americanum)*, 165, 201
Swamp rose *(Rosa palustris)*, 74
Sweet white violet *(Viola blanda)*, 153

T

Texas bluebonnet *(Lupinus texensis)*, 25, 122, 125, 170, 174, 175
Texas buttercup *(Oenothera triloba)*, 171
Thistle sage *(Salvia carduacea)*, 190
Tidy tips *(Layia platyglossa)*, 180
Tradescantia, 28, 30, 31, 41, 42
Trailing arbutus *(Epigata repens)*, 158
Tree cholla *(Opuntia imbricata)*, 66
Trout-lily *(Erythronium americanum)*, 158
Trout-lily *(Triteleia laxa)*, 109
Turk's-cap lily *(Lilium michauxii)*, 89
Twinflower *(Linnaea borealis)*, 161

V

Venus flytrap *(Dionaea muscipula)*, 87

W

Wake-robin *(Erigeron glabellum, E. glabellus)*, 99
Wake-robin *(Trillium erectum)*, 154
Water chinquapin *(Nelumbo lutea)*, 87
Waterleaf *(Hydrolea corymbosa)*, 165
Western buttercup *(Ranunculus occidentalis)*, 249
Western fringed gentian *(Gentiana dentosa)*, 231
White fringed orchid *(Habenaria blephariglottis)*, 219
White lady's-slipper *(Cypripedium candidum)*, 220
White-rayed mule's ear *(Wyethia amplexicausalis)*, 235
Wild bergamot *(Monarda fistulosa)*, 186, 189
Wild buckwheat *(Erigonum* sp.*)*, 175
Wild flax *(Linum lewisii)*, 180
Wild geranium *(Geranium maculatum)*, 156
Wild oats *(Uvularia sessifolia)*, 159
Wild sweet William *(Phlox maculata)*, 183
Wild teasel *(Dipsacus sylvestris)*, 189
Wine-cups *(Callirhoe digitata)*, 130, 175
Winter cress *(Barbarea vulgaris)*, 184
Wintergreen *(Gaultheria procumbens)*, 160
Wood lily *(Lilium philadelphicum)*, 158
Woolly lousewort *(Pedicularis lanata)*, 252
Wrinkled rose *(Rosa rugosa)*, 8

Y

Yellow columbine *(Aquilegia chrysantha)*, 227
Yellow fringed orchid *(Habenaria ciliaris)*, 219
Yellow goatsbeard *(Tragopogon dubius)*, 48, 183
Yellow lady's-slipper *(Cypripedium calceolus)*, 220, 292
Yellow lady's-slipper *(Cypripedium calceolus*, var. *pubescens)*, 83
Yellow pitaya *(Echinocereus dasyacanthus)*, 209
Yellow salsify *(Tragopogon dubius)*, 48, 183
Yellow skunk cabbage *(Lysichitum americanum)*, 195
Yellow trillium *(Trillium luteum)*, 155
Yellow trumpet *(Sarracenia alata)*, 215
Yucca *(Yucca arkansana)*, 175

Index

D

E

F

G

H

I

National Wildflower Research Center

The National Wildflower Research Center, a nonprofit corporation, was established on December 22, 1982, to stimulate and carry out research on the propagation, cultivation, conservation, and preservation of wildflowers in cooperation with universities, botanic gardens, arboreta, and other institutions throughout the United States, all aimed at enhancing the appreciation, use, and enjoyment of this abundant natural resource.